Santa's
North Pole
COOKBOOK

Also by Jeff Guinn

The Autobiography of Santa Claus

How Mrs. Claus Saved Christmas

The Great Santa Search

The Sixteenth Minute: Life in the Aftermath of Fame
(with Douglas Perry)

Our Land Before We Die: The Proud Story of the Seminole Negro

You Can't Hit the Ball with the Bat on Your Shoulder:
The Baseball Life and Times of Bobby Bragan
(with Bobby Bragan)

Sometimes a Fantasy: Midlife Misadventures with Baseball Heroes

Dallas Cowboys: Our Story

When Panthers Roared: The Fort Worth Cats
and Minor League Baseball
(with Bobby Bragan)

As told to Jeff Guinn

bestselling author of the Christmas classic
The Autobiography of Santa Claus

Jeremy P. Tarcher/Penguin
a member of Penguin Group (USA) Inc.
New York

Santa's
North Pole
COOKBOOK

Classic Christmas Recipes
from Saint Nicholas Himself

JEREMY P. TARCHER/PENGUIN
Published by the Penguin Group
Penguin Group (USA) Inc., 375 Hudson Street, New York, New York 10014, USA •
Penguin Group (Canada), 90 Eglinton Avenue East, Suite 700, Toronto, Ontario M4P 2Y3,
Canada (a division of Pearson Penguin Canada Inc.) • Penguin Books Ltd, 80 Strand,
London WC2R 0RL, England • Penguin Ireland, 25 St Stephen's Green, Dublin 2, Ireland
(a division of Penguin Books Ltd) • Penguin Group (Australia), 250 Camberwell Road,
Camberwell, Victoria 3124, Australia (a division of Pearson Australia Group Pty Ltd) •
Penguin Books India Pvt Ltd, 11 Community Centre, Panchsheel Park, New Delhi–110 017,
India • Penguin Group (NZ), 67 Apollo Drive, Rosedale, North Shore 0745, Auckland,
New Zealand (a division of Pearson New Zealand Ltd) • Penguin Books (South Africa)
(Pty) Ltd, 24 Sturdee Avenue, Rosebank, Johannesburg 2196, South Africa
Penguin Books Ltd, Registered Offices:
80 Strand, London WC2R 0RL, England

Most Tarcher/Penguin books are available at special quantity discounts for bulk purchase for
sales promotions, premiums, fund-raising, and educational needs. Special books or book
excerpts also can be created to fit specific needs. For details, write Penguin Group (USA) Inc.
Special Markets, 375 Hudson Street, New York, NY 10014.

Library of Congress Cataloging-in-Publication Data

Guinn, Jeff.
Santa's North Pole cookbook :
classic Christmas recipes from Saint Nicholas himself / as told to Jeff Guinn.
p.   cm.
ISBN 978-1-58542-589-1
1. Christmas cookery.   2. Cookery, International.   3. Santa Claus.   I. Title.
TX739.2.C45G85   2007   2007030724
641.5'686—dc22

Printed in the United States of America
1   3   5   7   9   10   8   6   4   2

This book is printed on acid-free paper. ∞

BOOK DESIGN BY AMANDA DEWEY
ILLUSTRATIONS BY HAVANA STREET, WWW.HAVANASTREET.COM

The recipes in this book are to be followed exactly as written. The publisher is not responsible for specific health or allergy concerns that may require medical supervision. The publisher is not responsible for any adverse reactions to the recipes in this book.

While the author has made every effort to give accurate telephone numbers and Internet addresses at the time of publication, neither the publisher nor the author assumes responsibility for errors or for changes that occur after publication. Further, the publisher has no control over and assumes no responsibility for author or third-party websites or their content.

For Jim Donovan

There are so many reasons why.

Contents

Breads *19*

Appetizers *43*

JULBORD (Christmas Board)   49

SILLSALLAD (Herring Salad with Potatoes, Apple, and Beetroot)   51

VARM RÖKT LAX MED SMÖR (Hot Smoked Salmon with Savory Butter)   53

GURKASALLAD (Cucumber Salad)   54
From Sweden

ATTILA'S STUFFED MUSHROOMS   56
From Germany

MISA DE GALLO LUMPIAS (Rooster's Mass Spring Rolls)   59
From the Philippines

FLAMING GINGERED PRAWNS   62
From Australia

SAINT FRANCIS'S *GALINHA DE PORTUGAL* (Chicken Wraps)   65
From Portugal

Main Courses 69

CHRISTMAS ROSEMARY TURKEY   75
From the U.S.A.

NORTH POLE BREAD DRESSING   77
From the North Pole

LARS'S RED WINE–REDUCTION GRAVY *80*
From the North Pole

WEIHNACHTSGANS MIT ROTKOHL UND GRÜNKOHL
(Christmas Goose with Red Cabbage and Kale) *82*
From Germany

TOURTIÈRE **(Spiced Meat Pie)** *90*
From Canada

HALLACAS **(Cornmeal Turnovers with Meat Filling)** *93*
From Venezuela

DORO WAT **(Chicken Stew)** *98*
From Ethiopia

CAPITONE FRITTO **(Festive Fried Eel)** *102*
From Italy

LEONARDO'S ***PASTA FRA DIAVOLO*** **(Spicy Seafood Pasta)** *105*
From Italy

LARS'S SAVORY POACHED SALMON *109*
From the North Pole

BULGOGI **(Fire Meat)** *112*
From Korea

LARS'S FAVORITE CHRISTMAS KEBABS *115*
From ancient Lycia (modern Turkey)

Side Dishes *133*

Drinks *161*

JULGLÖGG (Christmas Mulled Wine) *176*
From Finland

Desserts *179*

NONNA'S PATARA PUDDING *183*
From the North Pole

CHRISTMAS PLUM PUDDING *187*
From England

HOLIDAY PLUM PIE COOKIES *191*
From the North Pole

BLACK CHRISTMAS FRUITCAKE *194*
From Trinidad and Tobago

FRUITCAKE COOKIES *199*
From the North Pole

KAHK (Sweet Cookies) *202*
From Egypt

PAVLOVA (Holiday Meringue) *205*
From New Zealand

KULKULS (Coconut Cookies) *208*
From India

FOREWORD

Throughout the ages, there have been four essential elements that combine to create the special magic of the Christmas season. Worship is first among them. We're celebrating the birth of Jesus, after all. Then come family and friends. The holidays provide an annual opportunity to be with those we care about most. Gifts, of course, also play a major part. They symbolize love and generosity of spirit. Who knows that better than Santa Claus? For many centuries, it's been my privilege to share in the gift-giving excitement.

Then there's the fourth element of holiday joy—or perhaps I should say *ingredient*—and that's food. Can you imagine Christmas without those special meals and treats we look forward to all year? No matter where you live in this wide, wonderful world, when you celebrate Christmas there is always food involved!

I speak of this as an expert. During the extensive travel that the delivery of Christmas gifts requires, I've been fortunate enough to sample holiday fare in virtually every place on earth where Christmas is observed. Some of these dishes are traditional, meaning they are familiar to almost everyone everywhere, and others seem exotic to anyone who doesn't live and celebrate Christmas in a specific locale. Here at the North Pole, we relish them all. My waistline is proof!

It has always been my belief that the more we know about Christmas throughout the world, the more we will enjoy our own personal celebrations of the season. To that end, I'm pleased to share with you a selection of the finest holiday recipes from many different countries and cultures. Rest assured that we would never leave out traditional favorites like roast turkey and eggnog, but even in these cases we'll offer some intriguing new possibilities. Another dozen or so recipes come directly from the North Pole kitchen and reflect the history of cooking and Christmas through the lives and food-related experiences of myself and my beloved friends. Even if you haven't read my previous books—*The Autobiography of Santa Claus* (my life story), *How Mrs. Claus Saved Christmas* (thwarting Puritan attempts to outlaw the holiday in 1647), and *The Great Santa Search* (my modern-day struggle to remind everyone of the true meaning of Christmas)—you will have heard of some of them, like Ben Franklin, Saint Francis of Assisi, Theodore Roosevelt, and Attila the Hun. Over the centuries, these and other very special people have aided me in my gift-giving mission. Eventually we all moved to the North Pole, where we spend our days designing, building, and, on the holidays, distributing toys to children everywhere. We love every minute, though it's very hard work. But even the most enthusiastic Christmas celebrants have to stop and eat! With this cookbook, I'm so pleased to welcome you into our well-fed company.

As we begin, it's appropriate for me to properly introduce Lars, our official North Pole chef. Born in Norway midway through the twentieth century, he moved to St. Paul, Minnesota, with his parents when he was still a boy. Lars always loved to cook, and he became a well-known chef who operated his own restaurant. But he loved Christmas, too, and in particular wanted the holiday to be special for children who had no parents to celebrate it with them. So it became Lars's custom each Christmas to visit an orphanage just outside St. Paul, where he would create delicious holiday feasts for all the girls and boys. Lars based the meals on whatever ingredients might be at hand. He even taught several of the youngsters there how to cook these items themselves. After we heard about his exploits and went to St. Paul to meet Lars, we wanted very much to invite him to join us at the North Pole, with the goal of eventually sharing the secrets of his holiday kitchen magic with Christmas-season chefs everywhere. After his protégés assured him they would take over his responsibilities at the orphanage so the other children could continue enjoying wonderful Christmas treats, Lars agreed to come with us, and North Pole–based digestive systems have rejoiced ever since. Now yours can, too.

In the pages that follow, Lars has joined me in sharing with you the background of each particular dish. From good old classic American roast turkey (with an interesting twist or two) to the spicy holiday Ethiopian stew *Doro Wat*; from France's lip-smacking chocolate yule log, *Bûche de Noël*, to the Candy Cane *Crème Brûlée* that Lars invented right here at the North Pole, every recipe will add tasty enhancement to your seasonal revelry. You'll find some of these recipes gloriously simple, perfect for children who want to help prepare holiday snacks. A few will require considerable preparation, but they will reward you for your effort. I promise that all are delectable, whether they are consumed as part of a family meal or as potluck dishes at a jolly Christmas party. Everything regularly appears on our North Pole menu. Essentially, I'm inviting you and your loved ones to pull your chairs right up to Santa's own dining room table.

Happy holiday eating!

Breakfast

Families gathering to enjoy a delicious Christmas breakfast together seems just as traditional as everyone scrambling out of bed to see what presents I've left in their stockings and under the tree. In fact, we had "Christmas" long before any morning meal was called "breakfast." In A.D. 350, not long after I began my gift-giving mission, Pope Julius I formally declared that each December 25 would be set aside to honor the birth of Christ. Around 1038, people in England began referring to the twenty-fifth of December as "Christmas," basing the new word on "Christ's Mass." It wasn't long before English explorers and traders spread the term around the globe.

Like almost everyone else, I loved the word "Christmas" from the moment I first heard it, but the term "breakfast" was still four hundred years in the future. It was customary to eat a small, simple meal—fruit, bread, eggs, soup, things of that sort—to start the day. This repast had no real name until sometime around A.D. 120, when the Roman emperor Hadrian began distributing free morning meals to the poor; to eat this meal was known to the Romans as *disieiunare*, which is Latin for "to unfast." Over time, different cultures adopted their own variations of the term. It was altered to *disnare*, then *disner*, and in English, *dinner*. What we now call breakfast was once known as dinner! It was only in 1463 that an accounting book in England recorded expenses for "break fast," or breakfast. The term caught on; we've been enjoying breakfast in the mornings ever since.

Because Christmas morning is so special, it's only logical to make a special breakfast part of the December 25 fun. But what should it be? Many families will soon be on their way to church, so they don't have much time to cook and clean up. They want a Christmas breakfast that's quick and easy to prepare, though still delicious. Others will have more leisure and may enjoy breaking their holiday fast with dishes that take longer to make. Here at the North Pole, Lars and his kitchen staff excel at both.

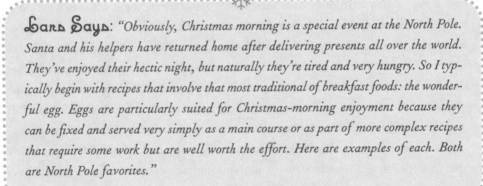

Lars Says: *"Obviously, Christmas morning is a special event at the North Pole. Santa and his helpers have returned home after delivering presents all over the world. They've enjoyed their hectic night, but naturally they're tired and very hungry. So I typically begin with recipes that involve that most traditional of breakfast foods: the wonderful egg. Eggs are particularly suited for Christmas-morning enjoyment because they can be fixed and served very simply as a main course or as part of more complex recipes that require some work but are well worth the effort. Here are examples of each. Both are North Pole favorites."*

Lars's Fluffy Scrambled Eggs with Rosemary

From the North Pole

PREPARE: *10 minutes* • COOK: *5 minutes* • SERVES: 6

There are few breakfast dishes that are quicker and easier to prepare than scrambled eggs. In the simplest version, eggs (probably two per person) are dropped in a bowl, beaten together, poured into a pan, and cooked for perhaps two or three minutes. Christmas morning clearly deserves something better, and the tasty scrambled eggs Lars always serves us are especially appropriate because rosemary is one of the ingredients.

Certainly, Christmas is about the birth of Jesus, but let's not forget his mother! "Rosemary" is named for the Virgin Mary. Legend has it that soon after Christ's birth, Mary and Joseph took their newborn to Egypt to escape the wrath of King Herod. Along the way, they paused to rest beside a green, wonderfully fragrant bush, upon which Mary draped her blue cloak. Overnight, the flowers on the bush turned blue, and the bush has been known as "the rose of Mary" ever since, though people shortened the name to "rosemary." Cooks soon began using finely chopped leaves and even whole sprigs of rosemary in many holiday recipes, including this one. Rosemary can be purchased at almost any grocery store, though you should really plant some in your home garden. It's easy to grow, and it perfumes the air!

12 eggs (two per person)
3 tbsp. half & half
16 to 36 fresh rosemary leaves, finely chopped
³/₄ tsp. salt
³/₄ tsp. ground pepper
6 tbsp. butter
³/₄ cup grated Parmesan cheese
6 rosemary sprigs (each 3 to 4 inches long)
  for garnish (optional)

1. Combine the eggs, half & half, chopped rosemary leaves, salt, and pepper in a small bowl and stir the mixture with a fork until blended.

2. Melt the butter in a 10-inch skillet over medium-low heat. When the butter has melted, pour the egg mixture into the skillet, stirring the mixture occasionally as it cooks. When the eggs are still somewhat runny (just beginning to clump together), add the Parmesan cheese and continue stirring until cooked to taste.

3. Divide the eggs among plates, and, if you like, garnish each serving with sprigs of rosemary. (Just stick the sprigs into the eggs at an angle.) We like to serve this dish accompanied by sliced pears. The rosemary and Parmesan cheese turn ordinary scrambled eggs into a richer, more flavorful dish.

Santa's Breakfast Soufflé

From the North Pole

PREPARE: *35 minutes* • COOK/BAKE: *75 minutes* • SERVES: *6*

When we gather at the North Pole for breakfast on Christmas morning, our holiday work is done. There's no reason to rush anything, including breakfast. So unless my friends and I have worked up unusually sharp appetites during our long night of gift giving, we are always pleased when Lars serves us delicious soufflés. These, of course, take some time to prepare, but the leisurely pace of an unhurried Christmas breakfast suits us—as it does many other families—exactly.

Lars Says: *"If you've never made a soufflé, you may feel a little anxious. It sounds quite intimidating, but the truth is that soufflés are incredibly easy to make. In this recipe, the only hard part is remaining patient while you prepare the cheese sauce.*

"Though I prepare these soufflés for Santa and his friends in individual soufflé dishes, if you prefer, you can place yours in a single, larger oven-safe receptacle and serve it in portions. Either way is fine."

9 eggs, separated
9 tbsp. butter
6 tbsp. all-purpose flour
1 1/2 tsp. salt
3 cups evaporated milk
3 cups shredded cheddar cheese
3/4 cup crumbled cooked bacon pieces

1. Grease the bottom of six 4-inch ramekins and place them in a shallow baking pan or on a rimmed cookie sheet. Pour enough water into the pan or sheet to reach a depth of one-quarter inch.

2. Separate the eggs, placing the yolks in a small bowl and the whites in a large mixing bowl; set the bowls aside.

3. Preheat your oven to 350°F.

4. Melt the butter in a medium saucepan over medium heat. When the butter has melted, stir in the flour and salt until the mixture is smooth. Gradually stir in the evaporated milk. Continue to cook over medium heat, stirring continuously, until thickened. Then stir in the cheese until it has melted. This is your cheese sauce.

5. Gently beat the egg yolks in the small bowl. Stir in a *small* amount of the cheese sauce until smooth. Repeat. Then *slowly* drizzle this mixture into the saucepan of cheese sauce, stirring constantly to prevent lumps. (You want a soufflé, not scrambled eggs!) Continue to cook over medium heat, stirring continuously, until the sauce is well mixed and thickened. Set aside.

6. Beat the egg whites in the large bowl until stiff. Gently fold in the crumbled bacon

and the cheese mixture. Pour into the ramekins, filling each three-quarters full. Using a clean, damp cloth, wipe any overflow from the edges of the dishes. Bake for 40 to 50 minutes, or until golden brown. Don't open the oven door while baking; if you do, your soufflés may fall.

7. Serve promptly for the nicest, most impressive presentation; soufflés do collapse fairly quickly. If you wait 5 minutes after taking the soufflés out of the oven, they'll still taste good, but they'll be only about half their original size.

Palacsinta (Pancakes)

From Hungary

PREPARE: *90 minutes* • COOK/BAKE: *25 minutes*

SERVES: *6*

Hungary is a land with many wonderful Christmas traditions and some of the most delectable holiday food! Naturally, several of these special dishes have become Christmas staples at the North Pole.

As it happens, Hungarian children expect me to bring my gifts on December 6, which they call Mikulás Nap, or "Nicholas Day," and I am referred to as Mikulás Bácsi, Uncle Nicholas. The boys and girls leave their shoes out overnight, and I fill them with candy. I also place other gifts beside the shoes.

But that doesn't mean Christmas isn't a special day, too. Children awaken to find more presents. These are brought by Jézuska (Baby Jesus) and his angels. After the gifts have been opened and admired, everyone enjoys a fabulous breakfast. Usually, this features *palacsinta*, savory pancakes that are somewhat similar to crêpes but much lighter, meaning you can comfortably eat more of them. This is exactly what I love to do when Lars includes *palacsinta* in our Christmas breakfasts at the North Pole!

Lara Says: *"You'll notice this recipe calls for something called 'baker's cheese,' which can often be purchased at specialty food shops. If you can't find baker's cheese, you can substitute large-curd cottage cheese, which must then be pressed through a fine sieve. That sounds like a lot of trouble, and in fact it is. But the pleasure you'll take in eating* palacsinta *makes that trouble worthwhile.*

"By the way, the proper pronunciation is 'pah-lah-CHIN-tuh.'"

THE BATTER:

5 eggs
3 1/2 cups whole milk
1/4 cup sugar
1 tsp. vanilla extract
3 cups sifted all-purpose flour
cooking spray

THE CHEESE FILLING:

1 tbsp. butter
2 cups baker's cheese, or 1 pint large-curd
  cottage cheese pressed through a fine sieve
2 eggs, separated
1/2 cup sugar

1 tbsp. freshly grated lemon zest

½ cup seedless white (some call them "golden") raisins, soaked in hot
  water for 1 hour and then drained

1 cup sour cream

1. Make the *palacsinta* first: In a large bowl, beat eggs well. Add the milk, sugar, and vanilla. Gradually add the sifted flour, beating until you have a smooth, thin batter.

2. Heat up a small frying pan or crêpe pan over medium heat. Coat the pan lightly with cooking spray. Pour in enough batter to cover the pan with a *very thin* layer, tilting the pan with a circular wrist motion so the mixture spreads evenly. The pancakes will cook very quickly, about 30 seconds on each side. To serve six, fix 12 pancakes.

3. Now it's time to prepare the *palacsinta* filling: Preheat your oven to 350°F. (Do this while you're making the pancakes.) With 1 tablespoon of butter, lightly grease an 8-inch-square ovenproof dish.

4. In a large bowl, mix the cheese, egg yolks, ¼ cup of the sugar, the lemon zest, and raisins. In a separate bowl, beat the egg whites until stiff. Gently fold a small portion of the egg whites into the cheese mixture, then fold in the remaining egg whites.

5. Place an equal portion of the filling on each *palacsinta*. Roll up the pancakes jelly-roll fashion and place the rolls one next to another in the prepared dish.

6. Heat the sour cream in a small saucepan, gently stirring with a whisk until it liquefies. Pour half the sour cream over the *palacsinta*, then sprinkle them with the remaining ¼ cup sugar. Bake for 20 minutes. Cover with the remaining sour cream, and serve at once.

Pecan Waffles for Våffeldagen

From Sweden (with a special North Pole twist)

✦

PREPARE: *15 minutes* • COOK: *3 minutes per waffle*
SERVES: *6 (2 waffles per person)*

Many people are surprised to learn that eating waffles is an important part of holiday-related celebrations in Sweden, where they begin the countdown to Christmas exactly nine months *before* December 25.

March 25, the approximate day in biblical lore on which the archangel Gabriel announced to Mary that she would give birth to the child of God, is celebrated in some countries, including Sweden, as the Feast of the Annunciation. In Sweden, March 25 is also celebrated as the first day of spring, when families want to commemorate nicer weather by enjoying some tasty food. And what food might that be? Waffles, of course!

Though the first people to prepare crude cakes pressed between hot stones were probably the Greeks, today's waffles and waffle irons come to us via Europe and Scandinavia. Waffles made their way to America thanks to settlers from the Netherlands. Although they were English and sailed from a British port, the Pilgrims who eventually arrived in the New World in 1620 had gathered for this journey in the Netherlands, where they developed a taste for waffles. It should come as no surprise, then, that waffles were one of the mainstays in their Plymouth colony.

One renowned figure in history, Thomas Jefferson, supposedly brought the first waffle iron to America from France in the late 1700s or early 1800s.

In Sweden, March 25 is now popularly known as Våffeldag, or Waffle Day, and the surrounding days as Våffeldagen. What a delightful name! I invite you to bring Våffeldagen to your breakfast table on Christmas morning in the form of these amazing pecan waffles, which Lars bases on a recipe he discovered in Stockholm.

> **Lars Says**: *"You need a waffle iron to make this dish; frozen prepackaged waffles won't do. If you don't have a waffle iron, you can find some good ones at relatively low prices in most department stores.*
>
> *"Parents, don't be concerned that the suggested ingredients include a bit of Frangelico liqueur. It's optional, and the alcohol content cooks completely away, imparting a light, nutty taste to the waffles.*
>
> *"We show this recipe as serving two waffles per person. Remember, we're at the North Pole, and Santa has a reputation to uphold. If your family enjoys smaller quantities than Santa, you can probably plan for one waffle each.*
>
> *"We like these waffles at the North Pole because they're delicious and very easy to make. Hurray for Våffeldagen!"*

3 cups maple syrup
4 eggs
3 cups half & half

$^1/_2$ cup vegetable oil
4 cups all-purpose flour
2 tbsp. baking powder
2 tsp. sugar
$^1/_2$ tsp. salt
1 cup finely chopped pecan bits
6 tbsp. Frangelico liqueur (optional)
marshmallow crème or powdered sugar (optional)
1 cup pecan halves

1. Preheat the waffle iron for 10 minutes or as the manufacturer directs; this is essential for crisp waffles.
2. Meanwhile, warm the maple syrup in a microwave or over low heat in a saucepan. Waffles taste so much better if you use warm maple syrup.
3. Combine the eggs, half & half, and vegetable oil in a large mixing bowl. Beat until thoroughly blended. Add the flour, baking powder, sugar, salt, chopped pecan bits (save the halves for toppings), and Frangelico. Continue beating until well blended.
4. Pour the batter into the hot waffle iron and cook for about $1^1/_2$ to 2 minutes, until golden brown.
5. Before serving the waffles, place three small dollops of marshmallow crème in the center of each—these will quickly melt—or sprinkle lightly with powdered sugar. Top the waffles with the pecan halves, and serve with the warm maple syrup.

Holiday *Avgolemono* Soup
(Egg-and-Lemon Soup)

From Greece

PREPARE: *about 45 minutes* • COOK: *1 ½ hours* • SERVES: *6 to 8*

Soup for breakfast? And on Christmas morning? Well, why not? Throughout history, all sorts of foods have been served for breakfast, and in Greece many families wouldn't think Christmas morning was complete without enjoying hearty bowls of avgolemono soup.

Christmas in Greece is such a very special time. On Christmas Eve, village children go from house to house singing carols, a custom the Greeks call *kalanda*. Grown-ups thank them by distributing treats of candy and dried fruit. On Christmas morning, most families attend church services—but not before partaking of this traditional breakfast!

1 whole chicken (3 lbs.), cut into 8 pieces
2 carrots, chopped
2 onions, sliced
2 stalks of celery, chopped
1 bay leaf
water
$\frac{1}{2}$ cup uncooked rice
2 eggs
juice of 2 small lemons
salt and freshly ground pepper

1. Place the chicken, vegetables, and bay leaf in a large pot. Add enough water to cover and bring to a boil. Reduce the heat, cover, and simmer for at least 1 hour, until the meat will easily pull away from the bone.

2. Strain the mixture, then return $7\frac{1}{2}$ cups of the stock to the pot. The chicken and vegetables are not needed for the rest of this recipe. Add the rice to the stock and cook for 25 to 30 minutes, until tender. Set aside to cool slightly.

3. While the rice is cooking, beat the eggs in a small bowl. Slowly add the lemon juice, continuing to gently beat the mixture; set aside.

4. When the chicken is cool enough to handle, remove and discard skin and bones. Cut the chicken into bite-size pieces.

5. Take 1 cup of the slightly cooled stock and add it, 1 tablespoonful at a time, to the egg-and-lemon mixture, beating constantly to prevent curdling. Repeat until the entire cup of stock has been blended in. Stirring continuously, add this mixture to the rice and stock in the pot. Season to taste with salt and pepper. Serve at once. You're experiencing Christmas morning in Greece!

Breads

I t should come as little surprise that bread is a menu mainstay in every country that celebrates Christmas. Likewise the fact that the bread recipes are as
wonderfully varied as the holiday celebrations themselves. Of course, bread itself is
one of the oldest known foods. Archaeologists have found evidence revealing that ten
thousand years ago people were baking and eating bread, albeit a very simple one made
from grains flattened with stones. A major breakthrough occurred around 2500 B.C.,
when bakers in the Mediterranean and Middle East began adding fermented dough to their
bread mix. By causing the dough to rise before baking, it produced significantly lighter
bread.

Bread is never quick and easy to prepare, but the preparation and baking process is a
perfect time for family or friends to gather in the kitchen to spend time together while sharing cooking chores. And, of course, there is no finer aroma to perfume a house and con-
jure a sense of well-being and contentment than the smell of baking bread!

If you would like to share Christmas baking experiences from around the world, the recipes that follow will provide some mouthwatering fun for you and your family!

❄

Lars Says: "I don't entirely agree with Santa that preparing and baking bread is never easy. It does take some time, but usually the steps involved are not especially complicated. In fact, I recommend bread baking as a perfect way to keep excited young-sters busy during the last days before Christmas. Christopsomo, *the first recipe here, even lets them try their hands at a little holiday artwork!*

"Many cooks like to use bread machines, but making these breads the old-fashioned way is a more authentic experience."

Christopsomo (Christ's Bread)

From Greece

PREPARE: *2 to 3 hours* • BAKE: *35 to 40 minutes* • SERVES: *6 to 8*

There is so much about Christmas in Greece that is unique, including the Greek version of Santa Claus. I'm Saint Nicholas there, as I am in many other countries, but in Greece I'm the patron saint of sailors, and, as such, children believe my beard drips with seawater and my robes are equally drenched!

A drier Grecian holiday tradition involves *Christopsomo*, a delicious bread flavored with cardamom seeds and full of white raisins and walnuts. Families often bake a loaf of *Christopsomo* together on Christmas Eve. A special part of the fun involves having children make designs from dough to decorate the top of the loaf before it goes into the oven. They might choose to represent their favorite hobbies and interests with rough images of books or bicycles or baseballs. Perhaps a figure of the family pet would provide the perfect embellishment. Anything, really, is appropriate.

Lars Says: *"Even though it's hard, try to stay patient enough to let the dough rise completely. If you don't, the resulting bread will taste a little bit dense and dry. And don't try to decorate the loaf until the dough has risen!"*

1 envelope active dry yeast
1/4 cup warm water
1/3 cup sugar
1/4 tsp. salt
1/4 cup milk
1 egg
1 tsp. ground cardamom
1/4 cup (1/2 stick) butter, melted
1 1/2 cups whole-wheat flour
1 cup all-purpose flour
1/4 cup golden raisins
1/4 cup chopped walnuts

1. Grease an 8-inch round cake pan; set aside.
2. In a small bowl, dissolve the yeast in the warm water. Allow to stand for a few minutes, until foamy.
3. Meanwhile, combine the sugar, salt, milk, egg, cardamom, and butter in a large bowl; mix well. Add the yeast mixture, both types of flour, the raisins, and the walnuts; mix well. If the dough is too moist, add just a little more all-purpose flour. You want a soft, smooth dough.
4. Turn the dough out on a hard, lightly floured surface and knead by hand until it is smooth and elastic. This should take 5 to 10 minutes. In a small bowl, set aside a bit of dough for designs; shape the remainder into a round loaf. Place the loaf in

the cake pan and cover both pieces of dough with a towel. Set aside to rise in a warm place until the loaf is about twice its original size.

5. While the dough is rising, preheat your oven to 350°F.

6. When risen, the loaf is ready for decoration. Bake the loaf for 35 to 40 minutes, or until it is golden brown. Allow to cool for 5 minutes before removing it from the pan.

Rosca de Reyes (Kings' Ring)

From Peru

PREPARE: *1 hour plus 70 to 90 minutes for resting and rising*
BAKE: *30 minutes* • SERVES: *12*

Christmas Eve in Peru is known as Noche Buena, the "Good Night," and it certainly is. Most children return home after Midnight Mass to find that I've come and filled their stockings with presents. But before these gifts are unwrapped, there's an important ceremony to perform. Peruvian homes are decorated for the holidays with elaborate manger scenes. The boys and girls can't unwrap my gifts until they have placed a tiny figure of the baby Jesus in his cradle. Only after the Christ Child is properly displayed can they finally see what I have brought them! I think this is a wonderful way to remind the young people why they are celebrating Christmas.

Holiday observances in Peru continue through Epiphany on January 6, when families often prepare *Rosca de Reyes*, or Kings' Ring, a tasty confection honoring the Three Kings, or Wise Men, who brought their gifts to Jesus on what holiday legend suggests was the sixth of January. You, of course, are free to bake *Rosca de Reyes* on any day you like; it's a great treat anytime during the holidays!

 *"One of the nice things about* Rosca de Reyes *is that you can make it well in advance. It tastes just as good defrosted out of the freezer. You might want to wait to add the icing until just before serving. There are many steps and ingredients involved but nothing especially complicated, which makes this recipe perfect for parents and children to fix together, and it's just right for having on hand as a Christmas-themed treat for guests."*

❄

THE DOUGH:

3¹/₂ cups all-purpose flour

1 envelope active dry yeast

²/₃ cup milk

¹/₂ cup (1 stick) butter, softened

¹/₃ cup granulated sugar

¹/₂ tsp. salt

2 eggs

THE FILLING:

¹/₄ cup granulated sugar

2 tsp. ground cinnamon

³/₄ cup diced candied mixed fruit

¹/₂ cup chopped toasted almonds

THE ICING:

1 cup sifted powdered sugar
¼ tsp. vanilla extract
2 tbsp. orange juice

1. Grease a baking or cookie sheet; set aside.
2. In a large bowl, mix 1½ cups of the flour and the yeast; set aside.
3. In a small saucepan, heat the milk, 5 tbsp. of the butter, the granulated sugar, and salt, stirring until warm. The butter should be almost melted. Add the milk mixture to the flour mixture and stir until blended. Add the eggs and beat with an electric mixer on low speed for 30 to 45 seconds, then beat on high speed for 3 minutes. Work in the remaining 2 cups flour with a spoon.
4. Place the dough on a lightly floured surface and knead for about 5 minutes, until smooth and soft. Cover and let rise in a warm place for 30 to 40 minutes, until approximately double in size. Punch down dough, cover, and let rest for 10 minutes.
5. Roll the dough into a 20 by 12–inch rectangle. Coat with the remaining 3 tbsp. softened butter.
6. Prepare the filling: In a medium bowl, combine the granulated sugar and cinnamon. Add the mixed fruit and almonds, tossing the mixture so the fruit and nuts will be lightly coated with cinnamon-sugar. Then sprinkle the filling evenly on the rectangle of dough. Starting on the longer side, roll up the rectangle with the filling inside. Moisten the edges of the roll with milk and pinch tightly to seal in the filling.
7. Place the roll *seam side down* on the prepared sheet. Pull the ends of the roll together to form a ring. Again, moisten the ends with milk and pinch tightly. Use a

sharp knife to make a dozen $^2/_3$-inch-deep cuts around the edge of the dough at $1^1/_2$-inch intervals. Cover and let rise for 30 to 40 minutes.

8. Bake in a preheated 350°F oven for 30 minutes. Remove the bread from the baking sheet and transfer to a wire rack to cool. You can cool the ring completely and freeze it if you prefer, or serve it right away.

9. Before serving, prepare the icing: Combine the powdered sugar and vanilla. Stir in the orange juice until smooth. This should result in a thin icing that can be drizzled over the ring with a large spoon.

Ben Franklin's Festive Blueberry Muffins

From the U.S.A.

PREPARE: *45 minutes* • BAKE: *20 minutes*
SERVES: *6 (2 muffins per person)*

Among all my North Pole friends, Ben Franklin is the greatest student of American history, and why not? He's a major part of it! In particular, Ben likes to remind us that not all holiday treats came to America from other countries.

In my centuries of gift giving, I have never met anyone anywhere who didn't love freshly baked blueberry muffins. These treats are bound to be a hit with family and friends. Ben is especially fond of them because, he points out, blueberries are one of the very few fruits native to North America. Long before European colonists arrived in what they called "the New World," Native Americans were using blueberries in soups and stews. Blueberries also were the main ingredient in *sautauthig*, the fabulous pudding that was served on ceremonial occasions.

We're not sure who first baked blueberries in muffins, but we're certainly glad he or she did. I'm pleased to reproduce here Lars's special blueberry muffin recipe, which he named in honor of Ben Franklin and always serves at the North Pole sometime during the holiday season. Santa Claus never exaggerates: I promise that these will be among the finest blueberry muffins you've ever tasted.

THE BATTER:

6 tbsp. unsalted butter

1 1/2 cups all-purpose flour

3/4 cup sugar

1 1/2 tsp. baking powder

3/4 tsp. salt

1/3 cup whole milk

1 large egg

1 large egg yolk (discard white of second egg)

1 tsp. vanilla extract

1 1/2 tsp. zested and chopped lemon peel

1 1/2 cups fresh blueberries

THE TOPPING:

3 tbsp. cold, hard butter, cut into 1/2-inch cubes

1/2 cup all-purpose flour

3 1/2 tbsp. sugar

1. Generously grease the cups of 1 standard muffin tin; set aside.

2. Place a rack in the top third of your oven. Preheat to 375°F.

3. Prepare the batter: Melt the butter in a small saucepan over low heat. (You want it barely melted, not cooked.) Remove the pan from the heat and cool slightly.

4. Combine the dry ingredients in a large bowl and whisk them until fully blended. Add the melted butter, the milk, egg, yolk, vanilla, and lemon zest and whisk until well combined, meaning that the flour and sugar are fully incorporated into the batter. Don't overmix! Very gently fold in the blueberries, making certain they're evenly distributed in the batter.

5. Spoon the batter evenly into the muffin-pan cups until all the batter has been used. With a damp paper towel, wipe off any spilled batter. Set the filled muffin tin aside.

6. Combine all the topping ingredients in a small bowl. Rub these ingredients between your fingers, breaking up the butter cubes and mixing them with the flour and sugar until the mixture becomes crumbly. This should take 3 to 4 minutes. Sprinkle the topping evenly on the muffins.

7. Place the muffin tin in the oven and bake for 18 to 20 minutes. When the muffins are golden and the topping a bit crisp, they're ready! Remove them from the oven, and let cool on a wire rack for 15 minutes. Only then should you run a thin knife around the edges of the muffins and remove them from the tin. They'll still be warm, and just right for eating.

Christmas *Karringmelkbeskuit* (Buttermilk Biscotti)

From South Africa

PREPARE: *10 minutes* • BAKE: *4 hours, 20 minutes (You read it right!)*

SERVES: *8*

South Africa is home to people of many faiths, and those who celebrate Christmas— about eighty percent—differ significantly in their forms of celebration. Those whose worship encompasses native African traditions, for instance, may light special fires in their homes, since fires are meant as signs to welcome strangers. Other churches may organize community carol singing or stage covered-dish suppers. My own role reflects such gladsome diversity: Some South African children expect me to bring my gifts on December 6, or Saint Nicholas Day; others, on Christmas Day; and still others, on January 6, or Epiphany. Because there is no December or January snow in South Africa, sometimes I arrive by bus!

I'm very glad to oblige everyone, particularly since many families leave out *karringmelkbeskuit* for me to enjoy after I've filled all their stockings. These are biscuits or rusks rather than cookies, and do take considerable time to prepare. I've grown quite fond of these tasty treats, and I was pleased when Lars began to include them on our North Pole menus.

In South Africa, an important part of holiday celebration is when neighbors visit each other's homes. *Karringmelkbeskuit* is usually served along with coffee or hot chocolate. If you make a batch, you'll find they're handy for Christmas-season drop-ins.

Lars Says: *"Usually adults enjoy* karringmelkbeskuit *more than children do, because these 'rusks' aren't really sweet-tasting. I like them best when I dip them in my cup of coffee or hot chocolate. This softens their rather hard consistency. Most people compare* karringmelkbeskuit *to biscotti. See if you agree."*

1 1/2 cups unbleached all-purpose flour
1 cup whole-wheat flour
1/4 cup sugar
1/2 tbsp. baking powder
1/2 cup (1 stick) cold butter, cut into small pieces
1 egg, beaten
1 cup buttermilk

1. Preheat your oven to 350°F. Grease a cookie sheet; set aside.
2. In a large bowl, whisk the whole-wheat and all-purpose flours with the sugar and baking powder. Add the butter and, using your fingers, work the butter into the flour mixture until it feels gritty. Gradually add the beaten egg and buttermilk,

stirring with a fork. The dough should be just moist enough to hold together when pinched.

3. Roll the dough into golf ball–size pieces. Place the balls about 1 inch apart on the prepared cookie sheet. Bake for 20 minutes, until the balls have turned golden brown.

4. Remove the cookie sheet from the oven, and reduce the heat to 200°F. Then return the *karringmelkbeskuit* to the oven for 4 hours. When they are done, eat them right away or store them in an airtight bag. They'll keep for several days.

Willie Skokan's *Kolaches* (Fruit Pastries)

From Bohemia (Czech Republic)

PREPARE: *45 minutes* • BAKE: *20 minutes*
SERVES: *6 to 8 (2* kolache*s per person)*

For centuries, Willie Skokan, the renowned Bohemian artisan, has been one of my most beloved helpers. As soon as we met Willie, we discovered he could craft fabulous toys out of the most basic materials. Willie also taught us how to prepare the favorite holiday delicacies of his homeland, none of which required any exotic ingredients or elaborate preparation. Like Willie and the toys he makes, the recipes yield amazing results from the most basic components.

At the North Pole, we enjoy *kolach*es all during the holidays. They're filling enough to make a most satisfying snack but not so heavy that they spoil appetites for dinner. They are also special enough to delight drop-in guests or to bring along to parties.

Most of the time, Lars takes traditional holiday recipes and adds his own exquisite touches. All the *kolach*-making details and instructions here, though, come straight from Willie Skokan himself.

1 cup sugar
1 cup vegetable shortening
1 tbsp. salt
1 cup hot water
1 cup cold water
1 (12.75-oz.) can evaporated milk
2 eggs
2 envelopes dry yeast
5 to 6 cups all-purpose flour
pinch of grated nutmeg or lemon rind
1 (20- or 21-oz.) can poppy seed filling, or cherry, blueberry, or lemon pie filling

1. Preheat your oven to 400°F. Grease a large cookie sheet; set aside.
2. Mix the sugar, shortening, and salt in a large bowl until blended. Add the hot water; mix until thoroughly blended. Stir in ½ cup of the cold water and all the milk. Then add the eggs and beat until blended. Mix in the yeast and the remaining ½ cup of

cold water. Then add 5 cups of the flour, and the nutmeg or lemon rind. Beat until a smooth dough is formed, adding more flour as necessary.

3. Let the dough rise in a warm place about 30 minutes, until it has doubled in size.

4. Punch down the dough and then roll it out on a lightly floured surface to a thickness of about $1/2$ inch. Using a 4-inch round cutter, cut out about a dozen *kolach*es. Using a large spoon, put a good dollop of poppy seed or fruit filling in the center of each pastry piece.

5. Place the *kolach*es on the prepared cookie sheet and bake for 20 minutes. When finished, remove to a wire rack and let cool for at least another 20 minutes. Then devour every last crumb!

Banana-Walnut Christmas Bread

From the U.S.A.

PREPARE: *15 minutes* • BAKE: *1 hour* • SERVES: *6 (1 loaf)*

People all over the world love banana bread, and those of us living at the North Pole are no exception. There's something about the chewiness of the fresh, warm bread and the pleasingly assertive taste of bananas that work well together.

Though bananas and bread have been with us for many centuries, combining the two is apparently a relatively recent concept. The first banana bread recipes appear in American cookbooks from the early 1930s. It was a tasty way to avoid wasting overripe bananas.

Being a master baker, Lars naturally made it his objective to create the perfect banana bread recipe, and he very well may have accomplished this with Banana-Walnut Christmas Bread. It's a perfect accompaniment for a breakfast dish or a scrumptious, satisfying snack. (I personally like a slice hot from the oven and slathered with butter—surely since fruit is involved there can't be *that* many calories.)

The holiday season always includes unexpected drop-ins who should be offered refreshments, and this bread is also just right at room temp for serving with coffee. Whether you share it with family or guests or just bake a loaf as a special Christmas treat for yourself, I think you'll find yourself turning to this recipe all December long.

Lara Says: *"Holiday breads call for extra ingredients, and, while traditional banana bread is delicious, I've found that the taste is improved by the addition of cranberries and chopped walnuts.*

"Trying this recipe will also result in one of the most mouthwatering aromas you or anyone has ever experienced. I promise that during the cooking process you'll have to shoo everyone else out of the kitchen, because they'll come running to find what's baking in the oven."

1 cup sugar
½ cup (1 stick) butter, softened
2 eggs, lightly beaten
3 very ripe bananas, mashed
1 tsp. baking soda
2 cups all-purpose flour
½ cup walnuts, chopped
½ cup dried or fresh cranberries

1. Preheat your oven to 375°F. Generously grease a bread pan, then dust with flour. Gently tap out excess flour.

2. In a medium bowl, blend the sugar and butter; cream together until you have a smooth paste. Mix in the eggs. Add the mashed bananas and stir until combined. Next, add the baking soda and then the flour, stirring until all the ingredi-

ents are completely blended. Add the walnuts and cranberries and stir gently to combine.

3. Pour the batter into the prepared pan and bake for 1 hour. Cool in the pan on a wire rack for about 15 minutes before serving; the bread will still be warm when you bring it to the table.

Appetizers

I f we compare the holidays to a fabulous meal, then December 25 is the main course, but the whole Christmas season is a time for enjoyment. Many families like to begin decorating their homes around December 1, which appears to be a global predilection. In Italy, for instance, families construct elaborate manger scenes on tables, and each day they move the figures of the Three Wise Men a little closer to the stable in Bethlehem. In many countries, I deliver my gifts on December 6, or Saint Nicholas Day, so stockings are hung (and, in some cases, shoes set out) well in advance of the twenty-fifth. Others expect me on January 6, or Epiphany, when the Wise Men in the Italian manger scenes finally reach their destination: the stable and Baby Jesus. And, of course, December 25 through January 6 constitutes the famous Twelve Days of Christmas.

Since holiday celebrations can span a month or more, and, as we've agreed food is an essential element in the enjoyment of the season, you'll need some less substantial but equally special Christmas treats in addition to the components of celebratory breakfasts and lavish dinners. Sometimes, tasty smaller dishes are just what holiday spirits require.

That's where appetizers come in. Certainly, the recipes you're about to read can be prepared as parts of a multicourse Christmas dinner, but they're equally enjoyable all on their own, whipped up individually for a seasonal snack or prepared together as a "tasting" menu for a festive holiday party. If you need to bring a dish to someone else's gathering, take along one of these appetizers, and your contribution will be the hit of the evening.

Lara Says: "At the North Pole, I like to give our Christmas treats an international flair, which is appropriate since so many of Santa's friends come from countries all across the globe. As you'll see, some of my favorite holiday appetizers reflect the lives and food preferences of very famous people who have gone on to join Santa in his gift-giving mission."

Queso Frito "Feliz Navidad" (Fried Cheese Triangles)

From Spain

PREPARE: *10 minutes* • COOK: *10 minutes* • SERVES: *4 to 6*

In Spain I'm known as Papá Noel, and by the time I come to deliver my presents on Christmas Eve, the holiday festivities there have long been under way. As in Italy, elaborate manger scenes grace most homes, and each evening families and friends gather for drinks and snacks.

By Noche Buena ("Good Night," or Christmas Eve), everyone is swept up in the tide of seasonal joy. Carolers march from house to house, singing praises to God for sending His son. Their songs are known as *villancicos*, and the singing often goes on until nearly dawn, which means I have to hurry to deliver all my gifts before the children jump out of bed on Christmas morning! But keeping late hours on Christmas Eve is the national custom: *Esta noche es Noche Buena, y no es noche de dormir,* goes the popular phrase: "This is the Good Night, and not a night for sleep."

So everyone is up and happy and hungry. When carolers finish singing outside a house, they fully expect to be rewarded for their songs with tasty snacks, the most welcome of these being *Queso Frito.*

2 eggs, beaten
2 tbsp. water
1 cup plain dry bread crumbs
salt and freshly ground pepper
12 ozs. cheese (either Monterey Jack or mozzarella), cut into ¹/₂-inch-
    thick 2-inch squares or triangles
3 cups vegetable oil for deep-frying

1. Cover a baking sheet with several layers of paper towels; set aside. Mix the eggs and water in a small bowl.
2. Place the bread crumbs in a pie pan and season with salt and pepper to taste. Coat each piece of cheese twice, first with the egg mixture and then with the bread crumbs. Then repeat. Place the double-coated cheese pieces on a plate and set aside.
3. Pour the vegetable oil into a medium frying pan to a depth of about ¹/₄ inch and place the pan over medium-high heat. When the oil is hot (375°F on a deep-fat thermometer), fry the breaded cheese pieces in batches of no more than four at a time. Fry the pieces for about 2 minutes on each side, until golden, using a slotted metal spoon to turn them. As they are done, transfer the fried cheese to the paper towel–lined cookie sheet to drain. Serve as soon as they're cool enough to eat.

Julbord (Christmas Board)

From Sweden

The Swedes love the holidays so much that they traditionally extend them beyond the Twelve Days of Christmas! Over one thousand years ago, King Canute decreed that Christmas feasting should last one month, so the official Swedish holidays end on January 13. The fun is only beginning on Christmas morning, when families gather to see what gifts I've left under the tree or, rather, what presents Jultomten has brought this year.

In many countries, I'm known by a name other than Santa Claus, but in Sweden children believe their gifts are delivered by a holiday gnome named Jultomten who lives in a barn the rest of the year. I don't mind, for every culture is entitled to its holiday traditions. Besides, the traditional Swedish *julbord* is so delicious that I always enjoy my holiday jaunts to that lovely country.

Most of us have heard of *smörgåsbord*, an all-encompassing name for a variety of tasty appetizers served during most of the year in Sweden whose main ingredient is quite often herring. People can make full meals of *smörgåsbord*, which is also true of *julbord*, the name given to the delicacies served during the holidays. Some of these, like *Sillsallad*, *Varm Rökt Lax med Smör*, and *Gurkasallad* may sound and even taste exotic, but holidays are especially joyful when we share the culinary traditions of other nations. In particular, if you're hosting a Christmas party, these three components of *julbord* would be perfect appetizers.

Lars Says: *"Obviously, the preparation of these dishes is a little tricky, and some of the ingredients take some tracking down. Still, make the effort! We don't have specialty food shops anywhere near the North Pole, but I'm never reluctant to travel by dogsled or sleigh to find the fixings for* julbord; *Santa and his friends hope I'll prepare it sometime during every holiday season."*

Sillsallad (Herring Salad with Potatoes, Apple, and Beetroot)

PREPARE: *20 minutes plus 4 to 6 hours for chilling* • SERVES: *8*

1 lb. filleted salted herring or pickled herring

2 cold boiled potatoes

1 Granny Smith apple, peeled and cored

1 whole dill pickle

3 whole pickled baby beets, drained

1 red onion

freshly ground black pepper to taste

3 tbsp. sour cream

2 hard-boiled eggs, chopped

1 tbsp. capers, drained

Lars Says: *"If you use filleted salted herring, soak the fillets overnight in cold water. If you use pickled herring, no soaking is necessary.*

"Most mainstream grocery stores sell jars of pickled whole baby beets. You may also find jars of pickled herring there. If not, any specialty food store should stock them."

1. Cube the herring, potatoes, apple, pickle, and baby beets. Don't worry about making perfect cubes; a general small cubed shape is fine. Slice the onion into thin rings.
2. Gently toss the herring, potatoes, apple, pickle, baby beets, and onion rings together in a large bowl. Then transfer the mixture to a salad bowl and season with pepper. Cover and refrigerate the salad for 4 to 6 hours.
3. Just before serving, mix in the sour cream and garnish with the eggs and capers.

Varm Rökt Lax med Smör (Hot Smoked Salmon with Savory Butter)

PREPARE: *20 minutes plus 2 hours for chilling* • WARM: *20 minutes*

SERVES: *8*

6 tbsp. butter, softened
juice of ½ lemon
2 tbsp. finely chopped fresh dill
2 tbsp. capers, drained and finely chopped
1 tsp. freshly grated lemon rind
pinch of lemon pepper or white pepper
2 lbs. smoked salmon
dill sprigs for garnish

1. Cream the butter with the lemon juice, dill, capers, lemon rind, and pepper. Shape mixture into a roll and wrap tightly in foil. Refrigerate until needed, at least 2 hours.
2. Preheat your oven to 425°F.
3. Wrap the smoked salmon in foil. Place on a cookie sheet and heat in the oven for 15 to 20 minutes.
4. Remove the sheet from the oven. Remove the foil and place the salmon on a warm platter. Garnish with the dill sprigs and thin slices of the Christmas butter. The butter mixture will melt; the resulting taste and consistencies are amazing!

Gurkasallad
(Cucumber Salad)

PREPARE: *20 minutes plus 2 hours for standing* • SERVES: *8*

1 large cucumber
2 tbsp. salt
⅓ cup cooled boiled water
pinch of salt
pinch of ground white pepper
2 tbsp. sugar
⅓ cup white wine vinegar
1 tbsp. chopped fresh dill

1. Wash and thinly slice the cucumber. Place in a bowl and sprinkle with the salt. Cover the slices with a plate that will fit inside the bowl. Weigh down the plate (a large can of tomatoes will do) so that the water (juice) is pressed out of the cucumber. Let stand for 2 hours.

2. Season the cooled boiled water with the salt and pepper. Add the sugar and vinegar to create a dressing; set aside.

3. Rinse the cucumber slices under cold water, then squeeze out as much liquid as pos-

sible. Place the slices in a serving bowl. Pour the dressing over the cucumber, and chill thoroughly. Just before serving, garnish with the chopped dill.

Lara Says: "Slice the cucumber as thinly as you can; that helps eliminate some excess liquid."

Attila's Stuffed Mushrooms

From Germany

PREPARE: *15 minutes* • COOK: *20 to 30 minutes* • SERVES: *6 to 8*

This is one of the absolute all-time North Pole favorites, an appetizer created by Lars in honor of my longtime friend Attila the Hun. You may be amazed that such a ferocious warrior joined my gift-giving mission, but this only proves that anyone can be changed for the better by belief in the generosity of spirit that defines the Christmas season. Much like Attila, mushrooms suffer from a bad reputation that is in a certain sense deserved. Only about five percent of all mushroom species in North America are edible; several varieties are incredibly poisonous. We know that mushrooms were being used for medicinal purposes as far back as 11,000 B.C., and that five thousand years ago Egyptian pharaohs loved mushrooms so much that they made it illegal for their nonroyal subjects to eat them.

Originally from Asia Minor, Attila and his tribe gradually swept into what would eventually be called Europe, fighting and pillaging all along the way. Mushrooms were handy food for warriors; they could be dried, carried in packs, and used as a tasty ingredient in campfire stews. Even after he stopped fighting and joined me, Attila still loved mushrooms. Sausage and cheese are his other favorite foods, so one afternoon at the North Pole, Lars combined these ingredients into a spicy appetizer that will be a highlight of your holiday season.

3 tbsp. butter

1 tbsp. vegetable oil

1/2 onion, diced

1 tomato, diced

2 cloves garlic, minced

16 to 18 large white mushrooms, stems removed and minced

salt and pepper

1/2 lb. bulk sausage (ground without casing)

1 tsp. ground caraway seeds

16 to 18 thin slices of Muenster cheese to cover the mushroom caps

1. Preheat your oven to 375°F.
2. In a medium skillet, melt 1 tbsp. of the butter with the vegetable oil over medium heat. Add the onion, tomato, and garlic with some of the minced mushroom stem. Season with salt and pepper to taste, and cook, stirring occasionally, until the mixture is soft. Add the sausage and ground caraway seed. Cook over medium heat, breaking up the sausage with the side of a spoon, until the sausage is well done. Remove from the heat and cool slightly.

3. Place the mushroom caps stem side up on an ungreased cookie sheet. Fill the hollow created by removing the stems with enough of the sausage mixture to create a small mound.

4. Melt the remaining 2 tbsp. of butter and drizzle evenly over the mushrooms and filling. Place a thin slice of Muenster cheese big enough to fully cover the filling on top of each mushroom.

5. Place the cookie sheet in the oven, and cook the mushrooms for 5 to 7 minutes, or until the cheese has fully melted. Remove from the oven and let cool for 2 minutes before serving. If Attila happens to be at your party, don't let him eat all the stuffed mushrooms himself.

Misa de Gallo Lumpias
(Rooster's Mass Spring Rolls)

From the Philippines

~

PREPARE: *45 minutes* • COOK: *25 minutes*
SERVES: *15 (2* lumpias *per person)*

C hristmas in the Philippines is an especially pious time. For nine days, from December 16 through 24, most Filipinos attend five a.m. church services popularly called Misa de Gallo, or "Rooster's Mass," a tradition that dates to the Spanish colonial period, when priests scheduled mass so early because Filipino farmers had to get back to their fields. The colonial era in the Philippines is long gone, but the Misa de Gallo remains.

There is hourly Mass on Christmas Day, so everyone can find some time in the midst of celebration to come to church. *Cumbancheros* stroll the streets singing traditional carols and folk songs. By then, their vocal cords may feel weary, because in the Philippines holiday celebrations begin all the way back in September!

Obviously, food is an important element of such long-term immersion in the holiday spirit. One of the staples is *lumpia,* an exquisitely delicious small meat-and-vegetable roll that is certain to become part of your own family's Christmas traditions once you give it a try.

Lara Says: "There are all sorts of lumpia *fillings, and Filipinos will variously insist that the right meat to use is pork, or beef, or chicken. It's really up to the individual cook. I prefer pork; I think it makes the tastiest filling.*

"Don't let 'lumpia wrappers' in the ingredients list put you off. These can be found in clearly labeled packages in any Asian food market and often in specialty food shops. You can track them down, I promise, and you'll consider the time spent well worth it once you taste the results."

1 tbsp. vegetable oil plus 2 cups vegetable oil for frying
1 lb. ground pork (or chicken, or beef)
2 cloves garlic, crushed
$\frac{1}{2}$ cup chopped onion
$\frac{1}{2}$ cup minced carrots
$\frac{1}{2}$ cup chopped green onions
$\frac{1}{2}$ cup thinly sliced green cabbage
1 tsp. salt
1 tsp. ground black pepper
1 tsp. garlic powder
1 tsp. soy sauce
30 lumpia *wrappers*

1. Line a cookie sheet with a double layer of paper towels; set aside.

2. Place a wok or large skillet over high heat; pour in 1 tbsp. vegetable oil. Add the pork and cook, stirring frequently (stir frying), until no longer pink. Using a slotted spoon, transfer the pork to a bowl and set aside.

3. Discard the fat from the pan, leaving a thin coating. Return the pan to the heat. When it is hot, add the garlic and onion and cook, stirring, for 2 minutes. Stir in the cooked pork, carrots, green onions and cabbage. Season with the salt, pepper, garlic powder, and soy sauce. Remove the pan from the heat and set aside until the mixture is cool enough to handle.

4. Place 3 heaping tbsp. of the filling diagonally near the corner of each flattened *lumpia* wrapper. Fold one side over along the whole length of the filling. Tuck in both ends and roll up neatly, keeping the roll as tight as possible, as for an egg roll. Moisten the other side of the wrapper to seal the edge. Cover the rolls with plastic wrap to retain their moisture.

5. Heat a deep, heavy 10-inch skillet over medium heat. Add enough vegetable oil (about 2 cups) to reach a depth of $1/2$ inch and heat for 5 minutes (375°F on a deep-fat thermometer). Slide 3 or 4 *lumpias* into the hot oil and fry for 1 to 2 minutes, turning them until all sides are golden brown. Using a slotted spoon, transfer the *lumpias* as they are done to the paper towel–lined cookie sheet to drain. Serve immediately.

Flaming Gingered Prawns

From Australia

PREPARE: *10 minutes* • COOK: *5 minutes*
SERVES: *8 (about 3 prawns per person)*

Now, *here's* a holiday appetizer that combines fabulous taste, ease of preparation, and spectacular presentation all in one! If that sounds almost unbelievable, well, so is Christmas in Australia!

Many of Australia's holiday merrymakers are descendants of British colonists, so in some ways their celebrations mirror those in Britain: Father Christmas is expected to deliver presents after everyone is asleep on Christmas Eve, and December 25 is a day when families and friends gather to celebrate Christ's birth. But Australia also has its own unique traditions, foremost among which is "Carols by Candlelight," a delightful event that began in Melbourne on Christmas Eve in 1937. Residents gathered outdoors, lit candles, and sang Christmas carols as their combined voices filled the starlit night sky. What a wonderful demonstration of goodwill among men, women, and children of all ages and races!

The event spread to cities and towns throughout the nation and it has become customary to sing that lovely ballad "Let There Be Peace on Earth, and Let It Begin with Me" for the evening's final song. That is truly the perfect Christmas sentiment!

Christmas Day in Australia, of course, begins with the opening of presents, but later it's time for food. Australian Christmas menus are strikingly different from ours. For most of us, Christmas is a winter occasion, but because of geography December 25 is summer in Australia. Accordingly, many holiday treats are cooked on outdoor barbecues and often consist of seafood, which is so common there. One North Pole favorite is Flaming Gingered Prawns, a Christmas treat we look forward to all year.

ᴸarᴧ Saya: "Once again, alcohol—in this case, a splash of gin—is part of the recipe. The alcohol is burned off in the presentation, which is, as Santa observes, spectacular."

1¼ lbs. medium king prawns (available at any
    seafood shop and in most specialty food stores)
4 tbsp. (½ stick) butter
4 green onions, finely sliced
2 tsp. finely chopped, peeled fresh gingerroot
salt and pepper
½ cup gin

1. Peel and devein the prawns. Rinse them in cold water, then drain and dry with paper towels.
2. Melt the butter in a large frying pan over medium heat. Add the sliced green onions and fry, gently stirring, for about 30 seconds. Add the prawns and ginger. Fry until

the prawns are cooked. (This should take only a few minutes; frying time will vary depending on the size of the prawns.)

3. Season the prawns with salt and pepper to taste, then pour the gin over them. You can bring the pan to the table before igniting the prawns. Do this by holding a match an inch or two *above* them. The vapor of the gin should cause the liquor to briefly ignite. Everyone will gasp twice in delight, first for the dramatic display and then for the taste.

Saint Francis's *Galinha de Portugal* (Chicken Wraps)

From Portugal

PREPARE: *20 minutes* • COOK: *30 to 35 minutes* • SERVES: *4*

Saint Francis of Assisi is one of the important figures in Christmas history. Before he joined my gift-giving mission, it was Francis who wrote some of the first Christmas-specific carols, because he wanted ordinary people to have special songs to sing as part of their holiday celebrations. It was also Francis who suggested manger scenes as a way of reminding everyone that Jesus came into this world as a poor child.

During his early life, Francis traveled through much of the known world, always preaching themes of brotherhood and generosity of spirit. Like most itinerant holy men of that time, he depended on kind strangers for food and shelter. Francis especially enjoyed his visits to those countries eventually known as Spain and Portugal, where Christmas festivities have been both colorful and heartfelt for many, many centuries.

Then as now, chicken dishes are extremely popular, both for taste and affordability. Many families in Portugal still raise their own chickens, and meals on December 25 often reflect this. Francis, in particular, is fond of *Galinha de Portugal*, Portuguese chicken wraps often served as special holiday-season delicacies. Lars is always happy to prepare these for our dear old friend, and the rest of us at the North Pole are quick to gobble them up, too.

1 red bell pepper, thinly sliced
½ large onion, thinly sliced
1 clove garlic, minced
1 tbsp. olive oil
2 tsp. ground cumin
1 tsp. ground cloves
1 tsp. ground cinnamon
salt and pepper
½ lb. sheep's milk cheese, very thinly sliced or shredded
4 skinless, boneless chicken breast halves, pounded flat
2 tbsp. butter
juice of 1 lemon

1. Preheat your oven to 350°F.
2. Toss the bell pepper, onion, and garlic in a large bowl. Drizzle with the olive oil, then sprinkle with cumin, cloves, cinnamon, salt, and pepper, and toss until vegetables are evenly coated.
3. Place the cheese in the middle of each flattened chicken breast. Then place some of the vegetable mixture on top of the cheese. Fold in the ends of the chicken

breasts and roll them up, enclosing the cheese and vegetables. Tie the rolls tightly with kitchen twine, to prevent them from falling open while they're cooking.

4. Melt the butter in a 10-inch frying pan over medium heat. When the butter is completely melted, add lemon juice. Place the chicken rolls in the skillet and, using tongs to turn them, cook 2 to 3 minutes, until evenly browned. Remove from the heat.

5. Place the rolls in a greased baking pan, and pour any excess butter–lemon juice mixture over them. Cover the baking pan with foil. Bake the chicken for 30 to 35 minutes.

6. Remove the pan from the oven and let the rolls cool for 5 minutes. Then transfer the rolls to a serving platter. Cut and remove the twine. Using a *very* sharp knife, slice each roll into several sections. Serve immediately.

Main Courses

Almost every Christmas-themed novel, movie, or play includes a scene in which families and friends sit down to devour a holiday feast. Delicious dishes of every sort weigh down a table that nearly sags from the sheer weight of all the splendid food, among which, in the center, rests the main course: a magnificent roast turkey.

Or, if the scene is set in some regions of Europe, it is a roast goose. If the story is about Italian families, perhaps it is fried eel. Should the protagonists be from Ethiopia, the featured dish could be a spicy chicken stew. Koreans might be enjoying thinly sliced beef seasoned with sesame and soy sauce.

Around the world, what's served as the entrée for Christmas dinner is as varied as the traditions for celebrating the holiday. I think that's a fine thing. Food is a reflection of culture, and the celebratory repasts chosen for December 25 tell us much about the people partaking of them. Often, their traditional recipes are governed by economics, but those who can't afford grander meats and fowls still find ingenious, delectable ways to enhance less expensive fare.

It may be that you'll want to use one of the recipes that follow as an intriguing change from your own traditional Christmas dinner. Or, if you just can't imagine *not* serving turkey on December 25, may I suggest you try some of these tasty dishes for other evening meals during the holidays? At the North Pole, we certainly find that gastronomic globe-trotting ensures the very merriest of Christmas seasons!

My friends and I always enjoy a hearty dinner on December 25, a highlight of which is Lars's presentation of a large, roasted-to-golden-brown-perfection turkey along with a companion entrée: a delicious roast goose. Tandem fowl reflects the history of holiday dinners in North America as opposed to those of Europe and Asia Minor. For centuries before there was a holiday known as Christmas, natives of North America celebrated special events by devouring turkey, while their European and Asian counterparts feasted on goose.

Some early European and Asian cultures celebrated "goose gods." The birds' migratory patterns coincided with seasonal changes that these people marked with celebrations. We know that the Celts, for one, ate goose at their ritual meals. As cultures evolved, goose remained a special food. Germanic and Scandinavian tribes ate goose to celebrate Jul, or Yule. British kings expected goose to be served at their Christmas feasts.

Across the Atlantic Ocean, goose was certainly available and eaten on occasion, but the wild turkeys indigenous to the North American continent were the preferred celebratory fare. For one thing, they were available year-round rather than just in certain seasons. We know that for the Aztecs turkey was mandatory on holidays. Native Americans served turkey-based stews to mark special occasions.

Turkeys first made their way to Europe in the 1500s, brought back by returning Spanish explorers. The "exotic" bird's popularity exploded through Europe and England. King Henry VIII of England officially signaled turkey's emergence as the holiday fare of choice by requesting it instead of goose for his Christmas dinner. By 1843, when Charles Dickens wrote the classic *A Christmas Carol*, in which Tiny Tim cries, "God bless us, every one!" the Cratchit family and Ebenezer Scrooge are about to tuck into a giant turkey, not a goose. Even working-class British families wanted turkey on December 25.

Today in the United States you can buy turkey year-round. It's harder to find goose, except during the holidays. Turkey is also the classic main course on Thanksgiving, since it was one of the foods served by the Pilgrims when they shared their famous dinner with Native Americans in 1621. Almost everyone knows that, but no one really knows where "turkeys" got their name.

Historians tell us that around 1530, English traders acquired some wild fowl from Turkish merchants, and when they sold their haul back in Britain they described them as "turkey birds." Others suggest that Columbus gave these birds their famous name. In 1492, the Italian captain believed he had landed on the coast of India rather than a small island. Columbus's mistaken belief was that the large indigenous birds he saw there were some species of Indian peacock. Since peacocks were known in India as *tuka*, Columbus identified the fowl with a version of that name.

I suppose it really doesn't matter how they came to be called what they are; turkeys are now a beloved Christmas tradition. Accordingly, we'll begin with a special North Pole recipe for a roast turkey and bread dressing (and then we'll follow that with a recipe for mouthwatering roast goose that you simply have to try).

Lars Says: *"Most people buy their turkeys or geese frozen, but if you possibly can, try to acquire a fresh fowl instead. Some grocery stores and specialty food shops can order these for you. A freshly prepared bird is just that much tastier, but if you must use a frozen one, these recipes will still guarantee you a memorable holiday meal. Remember to let frozen turkey or goose thaw completely—don't stick a bird in the oven with icicles still dangling from its drumsticks!"*

Christmas Rosemary Turkey

From the U.S.A.

PREPARE: *20 to 30 minutes* • COOK: *3 to 3 ½ hours* • SERVES: *8*

O ne of the advantages of Christmas turkey is that once it's in the oven, you have time for fun and family. The real challenge is to find some way to make your turkey a bit tastier, a little more exotic, than the norm. This isn't especially hard. Christmas turkey doesn't have to be mild or even bland. Lars's recipe is an easy way to delight your holiday guests with turkey that will prove memorable without keeping you in the kitchen all Christmas Day when you should be having your fair share of holiday fun.

Lars Says: *"We included the legend of rosemary in the Breakfast section of this book, so I'll simply remind you that this aromatic plant is linked with Mary, the mother of Jesus. Just as it enhances savory egg dishes, it also imparts a lovely, delicate taste to turkey. Here, we also add garlic, which might shock turkey traditionalists. All I can say is, try it! You and your Christmas dinner guests will be delightfully surprised."*

1 (18-lb.) turkey, preferably fresh, or fully thawed if purchased frozen
coarsely ground pepper (Use pepper grinder for best results.)

8 cloves of garlic, peeled
24 rosemary sprigs
¼ cup olive oil
2 tsp. salt

1. Preheat your oven to 325°F.
2. If you're roasting a turkey that was frozen and/or prepackaged, remember to remove the giblet pouches from inside the cavity, then rinse the turkey completely. Pat dry with paper towels. Be careful in the cavity; sometimes there are sharp bones sticking out.
3. Grind about 1 tbsp. pepper directly into the body cavity. Then place the peeled garlic cloves as well as the rosemary sprigs in the cavity. Then place the turkey breast side up on a rack in a large roasting pan.
4. Drizzle the turkey with the olive oil, and massage the oil over the *entire* bird. Don't forget to coat the legs and wings. Completely cover everything with a thin film; you want the finished, roasted bird to have crackly, delicious skin. Liberally grind pepper all over the turkey. Use as much as you like. Then sprinkle the bird with the salt.
5. Place the uncovered turkey in the oven. Cooking time varies with the size of the bird. An 18-lb. turkey should be done in 3 to 3 ½ hours, or when a meat thermometer inserted into the thickest part of the thigh (not touching the bone) reaches 180°F. The juices should run clear rather than red or pink. If the juice isn't clear, the turkey isn't ready.
6. When done, remove the turkey from the oven. Cover loosely with foil and let it stand for at least 20 minutes to set the juices for easier carving.

North Pole Bread Dressing

From the North Pole

❧

PREPARE: *45 minutes* • COOK: *40 minutes* • SERVES: *8*

What's alongside the turkey you serve on Christmas Day is almost as important as the turkey itself. There are as many types of turkey dressing as there are ways to celebrate the holiday, but here at the North Pole we have a special favorite, one Lars has perfected to the point that we just couldn't imagine our holiday feast without it.

The modern concept of "dressing," or "stuffing," as some prefer to call it, goes all the way back to the Middle Ages, when various sorts of fowl—goose, duck, and chicken as well as turkey—were considered appropriate fare for holidays and other celebratory events. In earlier times, rich people crammed their roasting birds with all sorts of exotic items: The Romans, for instance, are known to have stuffed a goose with smaller fowl. But the poor of the Middle Ages, who needed to get as much nourishment from each individual bird as possible, had fewer options, among which bread was the most popular. Placed inside the body cavity of a roasting bird, the bread absorbs the cooking juices and makes a tasty, filling accompaniment to the mouthwatering entrée.

The dish itself was popularly known as *farce*, based on the French word *farcir*, "to stuff." Around the mid-1500s, English cooks simply translated and served "stuffing." This term displeased some people, who didn't find it dignified or appetizing enough, so they referred to it as "dressing." Whatever you choose to call it, Lars's recipe is delicious and would be a highlight of anyone's Christmas Day banquet. It's quick, tasty, and isn't even cooked inside the turkey!

Lara Says: *"To get just the right flavor and texture, remember to use both white and wheat bread. Not only will the flavor of the dressing be more interesting, the color of the dish will also be enhanced. This is easy to fix; give it a try!"*

1 cup (2 sticks) butter
1 large onion, chopped
2 cups diced celery
3 cloves garlic, minced
¼ cup minced fresh parsley
2 tsp. poultry seasoning
2 tsp. salt
1 tsp. freshly ground black pepper
sliced white bread torn into small pieces (about 10 cups)
sliced wheat bread torn into small pieces (about 8 cups)
3 eggs, lightly beaten
2 (14-oz.) cans chicken broth

1. Lightly grease a large baking dish; set aside.
2. Melt the butter in a large pot over medium heat. Add the onion and celery; cook, stirring occassionally, for about 10 minutes, or until tender. Remove from the heat.

Add the garlic, parsley, poultry seasoning, salt, and pepper; stir until thoroughly mixed.

3. Add all the bread cubes and the eggs, stir until nicely blended. Slowly add enough broth to keep the dressing moist but not soaking wet.

4. Spoon the dressing into the prepared baking dish, and bake with your turkey during the last 40 minutes of roasting. The dressing will absorb the turkey aroma and will not be the least bit soggy or heavy.

Lars's Red Wine–Reduction Gravy

From the North Pole

PREPARE: *2 minutes (really)* • COOK: *45 minutes* • SERVES: *6 to 8*

I personally cannot imagine Christmas turkey without gravy. Some of my North Pole friends jokingly suggest each year that Lars serve Santa his gravy in a soup bowl, since I love it so much. That would be overdoing it—perhaps. If Lars would really like to do that . . .

But my point is, delicious gravy enhances the turkey. I know that many cooks are reluctant to make gravy at all. Just the thought of trying intimidates them. Yet it isn't that difficult. Other chefs believe gravy is bad for your health, and refuse to serve it out of consideration for the well-being of their guests. Lars, however, has perfected a red wine–reduction gravy that is both simple to make and reasonably easy on the cholesterol. The latter can be attributed to the substitution of chicken broth for almost all the turkey "drippings." You really can't go wrong with this recipe.

Lars Says: *"I love to serve this gravy with the Christmas turkey recipe that precedes it because both are seasoned with savory rosemary. 'Wine reduction' means all alcohol is cooked away. This is tastier and lighter than most traditional turkey gravies, and we think you and your guests will love it.*

"The right time to collect turkey drippings for gravy is about 25 to 30 minutes before the turkey itself is done."

3 tbsp. butter
¹/₂ small onion, minced
2 cloves garlic, chopped
1 tbsp. chopped fresh rosemary leaves
¹/₂ cup turkey drippings
5 cups chicken broth
1 cup dry red wine
¹/₂ tsp. red wine vinegar

1. About 45 minutes before you plan to eat Christmas dinner, melt the butter in a large skillet over medium heat. Add onion, garlic, and rosemary. Sauté for about 3 minutes, until soft.
2. Add the turkey drippings, which you can easily take from the pan in which the turkey is roasting. Then pour in the broth, wine, and vinegar and bring to a boil over high heat, stirring often. Reduce the heat and simmer, stirring regularly, for about 40 minutes, or until the gravy has thickened (you'll be able to tell).
3. Serve warm over your Christmas turkey and dressing. Happy, gravy-laden holidays!

Weihnachtsgans mit Rotkohl und Grünkohl (Christmas Goose with Red Cabbage and Kale)

From Germany

PREPARE: *30 minutes (about 10 minutes for the goose)*
COOK: *4 hours (2 ½ hours for a 12-lb. goose alone)* • SERVES: *6 to 8*

I find that serving goose on Christmas Day evokes a comforting sense of history and holiday tradition. It doesn't hurt that roast goose is also so delicious. Of course, roasting a goose is more complicated than preparing and roasting a turkey, especially if you haven't fixed goose before. But be adventuresome; you'll be glad you were.

You should be able to buy goose at most specialty stores during the holidays. They can also be ordered online and shipped to your home.

We're including recipes for the red cabbage and kale that traditionally are served with roast goose in Germany. You can certainly skip these and just make the goose if you prefer, but the side dishes add to the color and delectability of the main course.

Lara Says: *"During the holidays when they're preparing goose for a Christmas feast, Germans often make 'goose* Schmalz' *for spreading on bread. It's delicious! Remove the excess white fat from the goose before the bird is roasted. Place the fat in a small pot, and heat it over a very low flame. Add fresh marjoram as the fat melts. When the fat is completely turned to liquid (rendered), pour it through a strainer into a bowl, let cool, and then refrigerate. Later, spread it on bread, sprinkle with salt, and taste the results. This isn't the healthiest of snacks, but a little holiday indulgence probably won't hurt.*

"You'll notice that this calls for 'a handful' of parsley. Don't be flustered by the in-exact term. We buy parsley in bunches. For the goose sauce, I'm suggesting a fistful of parsley from an average-size hand.

"When preparing this goose recipe, it is critical that you follow the instructions to baste the bird every 10 minutes. If you don't, the skin will get too crispy, and the goose will be dry."

THE ROAST GOOSE AND STUFFING:

1 (12-lb.) goose
3 Red Delicious apples, halved and cored
1 onion
20 sprigs fresh thyme
9 ozs. pitted prunes

THE SAUCE:

neck and wings of goose
1 tbsp. olive oil
1 large carrot, coarsely chopped
1 large leek, white and pale green parts only, rinsed well and chopped
2 stalks celery, coarsely chopped
8 sprigs fresh thyme
1 handful fresh parsley
$^1/_2$ (750-ml) bottle dry red wine
3 tbsp. red currant jelly
salt and freshly ground pepper

1. Preheat your oven to 475°F.
2. Cut the neck and wings off the goose; set aside for your sauce. Remove the excess white fat for *Schmalz*, if you decide to make it.
3. Cut the apples and onion into small chunks. Stuff the cavity of the goose with the apples, onion, thyme sprigs, and prunes. Tie shut.
4. Place the goose, breast side up, on a rack in a roasting pan. Do *not* put the goose flat on the bottom of the pan. It should not roast while wallowing in its own grease. Put the roasting pan on the lowest rack of your oven to prevent the skin from charring, and roast, basting the breast of the goose every 10 minutes with fat drippings, for 1 hour. Reduce the heat to 385°F and continue to roast and baste for about 1$^1/_2$ hours. To test for doneness, poke the goose behind one leg with a fork. If the juices run clear, the goose is ready to remove from the oven. Let the goose stand for at least 10 minutes (20 is better) before serving.

5. While the goose is roasting, cut the meat off the goose neck and wings and chop into small pieces.
6. In a large skillet, heat the olive oil over medium heat. Add the carrot, leek, celery, and meat and sauté for about 10 to 15 minutes, until the meat is cooked. Add thyme and parsley, then gradually add the wine and simmer, occasionally stirring gently, for another 30 minutes.
7. Pour the sauce through a sieve set over a medium bowl, straining out all the meat and vegetables; discard the solids. Add the red currant jelly to the sauce in the bowl and season with salt and pepper to taste. Return the sauce to the skillet and reduce over medium-high heat for another 30 minutes.
8. Serve the goose with the sauce on the side and with the stuffing as garnish.

Red Cabbage

½ cup (1 stick) unsalted butter
4 lbs. red cabbage, shredded
 water
⅔ cup balsamic vinegar
4 tbsp. finely chopped apples
8 bay leaves
1 tbsp. sugar (some cooks prefer 2 tbsp.)
2 tbsp. whole peppercorns
4 to 5 whole cloves
salt, to taste
½ cup red currant jelly
freshly ground pepper

1. Melt the butter in a large pot. Add the cabbage, water, vinegar, apples, bay leaves, sugar, peppercorns, cloves, and salt and bring to a boil. Reduce the heat to medium and simmer, covered, for $1\frac{1}{2}$ to 2 hours, adding more water as necessary, until the cabbage is tender.
2. Add the currant jelly and salt and ground pepper to taste.
3. Serve warm.

Lara Says: *"This dish tastes even better if it's prepared in advance. Make it on December 24, let it cool down, then refrigerate overnight. You'll have a scrumptious holiday treat on Christmas Day!"*

Kale

6 lbs. kale
12 ozs. goose, pork, or chicken fat
3 to 4 medium onions, cubed
water
1 ½ to 2 tbsp. ground nutmeg
salt and freshly ground pepper

Lars Says: *"It can be difficult to find goose fat unless you buy a goose and scrape the fat off yourself. Pork fat can be substituted. Chicken fat can often be purchased at shops selling specialty Jewish foods. You do need to use some type of animal fat to obtain the proper rich undertaste to this dish."*

1. Cut the kale into small pieces. It will look like you've got a whole mountain of kale, but it shrinks significantly during cooking.
2. Heat the fat in a large pot over medium heat until rendered and hot. Add the onions and sauté until they become transparent. Gradually add the kale, stirring and adding just enough water to keep the kale and onions from sticking to the bottom of the pot. When all the kale is in the pot, add the nutmeg and the salt and pepper to taste. Reduce the heat to medium-low and cook, covered, for 1½ hours, stirring occasionally and adding water as necessary.
3. Remove the pot from the heat and drain the kale well. Serve immediately, or refrigerate overnight before reheating and serving the next day.

Tourtière (Spiced Meat Pie)

From Canada

PREPARE: *25 minutes* • COOK: *40 minutes* • SERVES: *4*

I do love Christmas in Canada, a country faithful to both its English and French traditions. You can't go anywhere there without finding yourself in the midst of some joyful celebration. In certain parts of Canada, descendants of immigrants from Germany still observe that country's Christmas customs. Native American tribes have their unique celebrations: Children of the Cree Nation, for instance, leave out small cloth bags rather than stockings for me to fill on Christmas Eve, and of course I'm happy to oblige!

I make my rounds there under a variety of names: Santa Claus, Saint Nicholas, Father Christmas, Père Noël. The act of giving gifts, the reminder that generosity of spirit is the true theme of the holidays, is the important thing. And when all the presents I've left have been opened, families often head to the kitchen and begin preparing *tourtière*, a delicious, easy-to-make meat pie that is the centerpiece of many Canadian Christmas dinners.

1 lb. lean ground pork

$^1/_2$ lb. lean ground beef

1 onion, diced

1 clove garlic, minced

$^1/_2$ cup water

$1^1/_2$ tsp. salt

$^1/_2$ tsp. dried thyme, crushed

$^1/_4$ tsp. ground sage

$^1/_4$ tsp. freshly ground black pepper

$^1/_8$ tsp. ground cloves

store-bought pastry for 1 (9-inch) double-crust pie (or feel free to make
   your own piecrust!)

1. Preheat your oven to 425°F.
2. In a medium saucepan, combine the pork, beef, onion, garlic, water, salt, thyme, sage, black pepper, and cloves. Cook over medium heat, stirring occasionally, until the mixture begins to boil. Reduce the heat to very low and simmer for 5 to 6 minutes, until the meat is cooked through.
3. Line a 9-inch pie plate with pastry, leaving a 1-inch overhang. Using a large spoon, fill the pie shell with the meat mixture. Cover with the remaining pastry, folding the edges under and pinching them together tightly. With a small sharp knife, cut slits in the top crust to allow steam to escape. Cover the edges of the pie with foil and bake for 20 minutes. Remove the foil and bake for another 20 minutes. The crust should turn golden brown.
4. Remove the pie from the oven and let cool for about 10 minutes before serving. This is very important!

Hallacas (Cornmeal Turnovers with Meat Filling)

From Venezuela

PREPARE: *2 days (really!)* • COOK: *3 hours*
SERVES: *6 to 8 (3 or 4* hallacas *per person)*

D on't you find that the last few days before Christmas can sometimes seem to last forever? We're so excited about the holiday and so anxious for it to arrive that waiting patiently is simply impossible. Well, if you choose to serve your family *hallacas*, the traditional Christmas fare of Venezuela, then you'll have a delightful way of keeping busy as you wait for the calendar to finally turn to December 25. True, this recipe is extremely complex—it involves lots of ingredients and more than an average number of steps to prepare—but the result is worth it. Venezuelans would attest to that!

In Venezuela, holiday celebrations begin on December 16, when families put out their manger scenes. Though these have all the usual elements—Jesus in the manger, Mary and Joseph beside him, the Three Wise Men and their camels—some families like to augment tradition with modern touches like toy race cars or plastic action figures. No disrespect is intended. The idea is that they are mingling their own lives and interests together with worship of Jesus. I, for one, thoroughly approve!

And in Venezuela, most families and friends gather on Christmas Eve, or Noche Buena, for their main holiday meal, which almost always includes *hallacas*. Then everyone is off to Midnight Mass. Afterward, children hurry to bed so that Baby Jesus can bring them gifts to be opened on Christmas morning.

Lara Says: "I have heard people refer to hallacas as Venezuelan tamales. Try them, and you'll never settle for ordinary tamales again. The reason we suggest two days of preparation time is to make the process less stressful. If you like, you can certainly do everything together, but the various components can be prepared and then stored for a day or even two without losing any flavor or freshness.

"You may have to visit a specialty food store to purchase some of the ingredients called for here, but nothing should be particularly difficult to find. Still, I have two suggestions concerning the traditional ingredients. First, mustard pickle relish can be hard to find, so feel free to substitute the plain hot dog relish stocked in most grocery stores; it works just as well. Second, in Venezuela thin strips of corn husk are used to tie the hallacas shut during steaming, but kitchen string is fine, too.

"One last suggestion: Hallacas taste wonderful even if they're lukewarm, but they're at their absolute best when served piping hot."

THE MEAT FILLING:

1 lb. beef top round steak, cut into ¹/₄-inch cubes

1 lb. lean pork, cut into ¹/₄-inch cubes

¹/₄ lb. bacon strips, cut into ¹/₂-inch pieces

3 medium tomatoes, peeled, seeded, and coarsely chopped

1 onion, coarsely chopped

3 cloves garlic, coarsely chopped

salt

2 tsp. dried marjoram

1 medium leek, white and pale green parts, chopped

$^1/_4$ cup capers, drained and rinsed

1 tbsp. mustard pickle relish or hot dog relish

$^1/_4$ cup red wine vinegar

1 bell pepper, cut into $^1/_4$-inch cubes

1 tsp. Worcestershire sauce

$1^1/_2$ tbsp. dark brown sugar

freshly ground pepper

$^1/_2$ cup raisins

THE MASA DOUGH:

$^2/_3$ cup lard or vegetable shortening

1 tsp. annatto (achiote) seeds

2 cups masa harina

1 tsp. salt

1 tsp. cayenne pepper

$1^1/_3$ cups warm water

ASSEMBLY:

24 dried corn husks, or 24 (9-inch) squares of parchment paper,
    or 24 (9-inch) squares of foil

1 lb. shredded cooked chicken
4 hard-boiled eggs, sliced
¼ cup blanched almonds, chopped
2 ozs. sliced pimientos
5 ozs. pimiento-stuffed olives, halved
hot pepper sauce

1. Prepare the meat filling: Combine the beef, pork, and bacon in a large skillet.
2. In a food processor with the metal blade attached, puree the tomatoes, onion, and garlic. Add the mixture to the meat in the pan along with 1 tablespoon salt, the marjoram, and leek. Cover and bring to a boil over high heat. Reduce the heat and simmer gently for about 2 hours, until the meat is tender.
3. Add the capers, mustard pickle relish or hot dog relish, vinegar, bell pepper, Worcestershire, sugar, and salt and pepper to taste and bring to a boil over high heat. Cook, stirring constantly, for about 20 minutes, until just about all the liquid is gone.
4. Add the raisins and set aside to cool. If you prefer, cover and refrigerate for up to 24 hours.
5. Prepare the dough: In a small saucepan, melt ⅓ cup of the lard or vegetable shortening with the annatto seeds over low heat.
6. Meanwhile, in a medium bowl, using a handheld electric mixer, whip the remaining ⅓ cup lard or shortening until fluffy. Beat in the masa harina, salt, cayenne and water.
7. With a slotted spoon, remove the annatto seeds from the melted lard and discard

them. Add the melted lard to the whipped lard and stir until well blended. Form the resulting dough into 24 balls.

8. Assemble the *hallacas*: Place 1 ball of masa dough in the center of each corn husk (or parchment, or foil square). Flatten the dough to a thickness of about $\frac{1}{8}$ inch. Top each dough square with an equal amount of meat mixture, chicken, hard-boiled egg, almonds, pimientos, and olives. Don't be tempted to overstuff! Sprinkle with hot pepper sauce to taste.

9. Fold opposite ends of the corn husks (or parchment paper or foil) over the filling, completely enclosing it. Tie each *hallaca* snugly with corn husk strips or kitchen string.

10. Arrange the *hallacas* in a single layer in a steamer basket or on a rack over simmering water. Cover and steam for 1 hour. Serve very hot. If you've prepared and then frozen them a day or two in advance, they taste just fine when thawed and steamed.

Doro Wat (Chicken Stew)

From Ethiopia

PREPARE: *45 minutes*

COOK: *2 hours, or 3 hours if you're preparing* niter kebbeh

SERVES: *8*

Some of the most venerable Christmas traditions anywhere can be found in Ethiopia and for the most logical reason: It is one of the very oldest Christian nations, dating back to about A.D. 330. I was still a bishop and just embarking on my gift-giving mission when Ethiopians embraced the church. In the centuries since, they've joyfully celebrated Ganna, which is their term for Christmas. Just like the rest of us, they are glad to give thanks to God for His son, and to mark the annual occasion with music and fine food.

There are, however, some differences. Ganna is January 7, not December 25, because Ethiopia follows the Coptic Church calendar, which differs from our own. I'm expected to bring only small, simple gifts for the children, and when families go to church on Ganna it is traditional for everyone to wear white clothing. Two weeks after Ganna, there is a three-day celebration known as Timkat, for which children dress up in crowns and robes and march together through the streets to the accompaniment of percussive music provided by sistrums, which are gourd-shaped rattles.

Another difference is that the Ethiopian holiday commences with a forty-day period of limited fasting, so by the time Ganna arrives everyone is ready to feast! Spicy *Doro Wat* is as traditional a holiday main course in Ethiopia as roast turkey is in America. After you sample it, you're likely to add *Doro Wat* to your own family's Christmas traditions.

Lars Says: *"You'll see something called* niter kebbeh *listed as one of the ingredients for this dish. After the main* Doro Wat *recipe, we'll include one for* niter kebbeh. *If you don't want to go to the extra trouble, substitute butter. I certainly wouldn't blame you!*

"There are several unusual spices that are also necessary, but you ought to be able to find these in specialty food shops. Locating berbere spice can be tricky, so if all else fails track it down online and order it there.

"When Santa told me about Ethiopians and Doro Wat, *I was initially rather reluctant to give it a try in our North Pole kitchen. Chicken stew just didn't strike me as special enough to serve during the holiday season. But this recipe is not only delicious; it's also a reminder that Christmas is celebrated all over the world, not just in the more familiar parts of it. Now I delight Santa and his friends with* Doro Wat *at least once every December. They always ask for second helpings, and your family and friends will, too."*

juice of 1 lemon
2 tsp. salt
1 (3-lb.) chicken, cut into 8 serving pieces
2 onions, finely chopped
4 tbsp. niter kebbeh *(recipe follows or substitute butter)*
4 cloves garlic, finely chopped
1 tsp. chopped, peeled fresh gingerroot
¹/₂ tsp. ground fenugreek
¹/₂ tsp. ground cardamom
¹/₂ tsp. ground nutmeg
¹/₂ tsp. berbere
1 cup chicken broth
8 whole hard-boiled eggs,
    peeled and pierced with toothpicks

1. Combine the lemon juice, 1 tsp. of the salt, and the chicken pieces in a large bowl, preferably glass, and toss until the chicken is evenly coated. Set aside to marinate for at least 1 hour.

2. Meanwhile, cook the onion over medium heat in a *very* large pot, stirring constantly; you don't want it to burn. Reduce the heat and stir in the *niter kebbeh* (or butter), garlic, gingerroot, fenugreek, cardamom, nutmeg, remaining 1 tsp. salt, and berbere. Simmer, stirring occasionally, for several minutes. The onions should be soft and translucent but *not* brown.

3. Add the broth and bring the mixture to a boil, stirring gently. Reduce the heat

and add the chicken pieces, making sure they are completely covered by the sauce. Cover and simmer, turning each chicken piece several times, for 20 minutes. Add the hard-boiled eggs, making sure the sauce covers the eggs, too, and cook, turning the chicken a few more times, for another 20 minutes, or until the chicken is done.

NITER KEBBEH
2 cups (4 sticks) butter
4 tbsp. chopped onion
1 1/2 tbsp. finely chopped garlic
2 tsp. grated, peeled fresh gingerroot
1/2 tsp. ground turmeric
2 to 4 crushed cardamom seeds
1 cinnamon stick
2 to 3 whole cloves
1/8 tsp. ground nutmeg

1. Melt the butter in a saucepan over low heat, then bring to a boil. Add the remaining ingredients and simmer, *uncovered,* over low heat for about 45 minutes, until the surface is transparent and the solids have settled on the bottom.
2. Pour off the clear liquid and strain through a double layer of damp cheesecloth. Discard the solids. Cover and refrigerate the liquid until it solidifies. You've made *niter kebbeh*!

Capitone Fritto (Festive Fried Eel)

From Italy

~❧~

PREPARE: *75 minutes* • COOK: *15 minutes* • SERVES: *8*

No one is certain of the exact date of Jesus' birth. Many people don't realize that we celebrate Christmas on December 25 thanks to the Roman emperors Aurelian and Constantine. While many ancient cultures celebrated the winter solstice, it was the Romans who eventually blended several non-Christian traditions into one memorable holiday.

The Romans often changed or adapted their official national faith; when they would conquer a nation, they would sometimes absorb some or all of its religion, too. At one point, Rome renamed a Greek god Saturn and staged a weeklong winter solstice celebration called Saturnalia in his honor: During the week of December 17 to 24, people would feast and sing and give each other small gifts. When Emperor Aurelian wanted his subjects to worship Persia's sun gods, he proclaimed December 25 the Dies Natalis Invicti Solis, or Day of the Birth of the Invincible Sun, because Mithras, the Persian god of light, was supposedly born that day. Then Emperor Constantine changed the religion of the Roman state to Christianity. Since December 25 was already a holiday, he appropriated it in honor of Jesus. In A.D. 350, Pope Julius officially declared that all Christians would observe December 25 as a day of giving thanks for the birth of God's son.

So Christmas traditions in Italy date back to a time before there even *was* Christmas. And it's not surprising that today many Italians mark the day with feasts featuring seafood; their boot-shaped country is nearly surrounded by water. Beef was less common, and therefore more expensive than *frutti di mare*, or "fruits of the sea." So working-class families learned how to prepare seafood in especially delicious ways.

This brings us to *Capitone Fritto*, one of the most popular holiday dishes in Italy. Many of us seldom eat eel, but it's been served as part of celebratory meals for centuries. If you're ready to hark back to the very earliest Christmas feasts, give this recipe a try.

Lara Says: "In America, it can be difficult to find eel in stores. Your best bet is to go to a fishmonger or an Asian specialty food shop. Once you find it and fix Capitone Fritto, *which is quite easy to prepare, you'll understand why Italians have loved this festive dish for so long."*

2 lbs. eel
3 cloves garlic, peeled
salt and pepper
2 tbsp. olive oil
1 tbsp. red wine vinegar
$\frac{1}{2}$ bay leaf per piece of eel
all-purpose flour for dredging
oil for deep-frying

1. Cut the eel crosswise into pieces about 3 inches long. Wash, pat dry, and rub with the garlic cloves. Season to taste with salt and pepper, and drizzle with 1 tbsp. of the oil and all of the vinegar. Set aside to marinate for 1 hour.
2. Drizzle the eel with the remaining 1 tbsp. oil and dot with pieces of bay leaf. Then roll the eel in flour until well coated.
3. Fry the eel in moderately hot oil until browned and crisp. Drain well on absorbent paper and serve piping hot.

Leonardo's *Pasta Fra Diavolo* (Spicy Seafood Pasta)

From Italy

PREPARE: *25 minutes* • COOK: *1½ hours* • SERVES: *6 to 8*

Perhaps you want to celebrate Christmas with a festive Italian seafood dish that doesn't include eel. In that case, I'm pleased to recommend a recipe that's dear to the heart of one of my beloved North Pole friends, Leonardo da Vinci, one of the greatest geniuses who ever lived. Some know him only as a master artist. (Can there be anyone who hasn't heard of the *Mona Lisa* or *The Last Supper?*) But Leonardo was also an inventor; he filled notebooks with sketches of flying machines and two-wheeled conveyances that we call "bicycles" today. He even found a way to make Santa's sleigh fly, a story I've told in my autobiography. One of Leonardo's most lasting contributions to our gift-giving mission, though, is his mother's recipe for *Pasta Fra Diavolo*, a dish that is topped with a fabulous seafood sauce.

Leonardo was born in 1452 in the small Italian village of Anchiano. When he was still a young boy, he moved to the nearby town of Vinci, which is where he got the second part of his famous name: Leonardo *of* Vinci. If you travel to Vinci today, you may visit a wonderful museum that displays some of his notebooks, which include his first sketches of bicycles.

Utilizing the fresh fish that came from nearby waters, Leonardo's family created a wonderful, spicy pasta dish that helped make the holidays especially tasty occasions.

ℒara Says: *"Several different types of seafood are called for in this recipe. Some stores sell what is called 'a fresh seafood medley,' or a mix of fish, shellfish, and calamari, which is fine to use. If someone in your family objects to a specific ingredient, or if your favorite store is out of something that day—say, mussels or shrimp—you can eliminate it from the recipe without shortchanging the flavor of the finished dish.*

"This is a hearty dish, with lots of spice and a tangy flavor, so you won't need much in the way of appetizers or side dishes. Make Pasta Fra Diavolo *with the pasta of your choice. At the North Pole, we prefer linguini."*

3 tbsp. olive oil

2 cloves garlic, finely minced

4 Roma tomatoes

1 (28-oz.) can diced tomatoes

1/2 large onion, minced

2 tbsp. butter

salt and freshly ground pepper

2 cups dry red wine

1 1/2 cups dry white wine

1 (12-oz.) can tomato paste

2 tbsp. chopped fresh parsley

2 tbsp. chopped fresh basil

3 tbsp. crushed red pepper

1 tbsp. crushed fresh thyme

2 $1/2$ tsp. cayenne pepper

1 $1/2$ cups water

$1/2$ lb. mussels, scrubbed and "beards" removed

$1/3$ lb. tuna fillet

$1/3$ lb. bass fillet

$1/3$ lb. salmon fillet

$1/3$ lb. medium shrimp, peeled and deveined

$1/3$ lb. sea scallops

$1/3$ lb. calamari

1 16-oz. package dried pasta of your choice

1. In a large deep skillet or Dutch oven, heat 2 tbsp. of the oil over medium heat until hot. Add half the garlic and cook until it just begins to brown. Add the Roma tomatoes, diced tomatoes, onion, butter, and a pinch of salt and pepper and cook until the tomatoes begin to fall apart. Add the red wine and continue to cook for several minutes. Add the white wine, tomato paste, all the herbs and spices, the remaining garlic, and the remaining 1 tbsp. oil. Reduce the heat to low and simmer, stirring frequently, for 30 minutes.

2. Meanwhile, bring a large pot of water to boil for the pasta.

3. Transfer $3/4$ cup of the sauce base to a blender and puree until smooth. Transfer the pureed sauce to the bottom of a large soup pot or steamer. Add the water and heat over high heat until the liquid steams.

4. Add the mussels to the steamer basket or rack and place in the pot (or place the mussels directly in the liquid). Cover and steam for 3 minutes. The mussels are ready when their shells are fully open. (Any mussels with unopened shells are bad and should be discarded.) Remove the mussels from the steamer or soup pot and drain.

5. Add all the remaining seafood to the base sauce, and simmer over low heat for about 10 minutes.

6. Meanwhile, cook the pasta as directed on the package label. When it is just *al dente* (slightly chewy), drain well and divide among pasta bowls. Ladle the *Fra Diavolo* sauce over the pasta and garnish each plate with some of the steamed mussels. Leonardo will wish he were sharing this holiday feast with you!

Lars's Savory Poached Salmon

From the North Pole

❧

PREPARE: *10 minutes* • COOK: *15 minutes* • SERVES: *4 to 6*

It's inevitable that sometime during the holidays you'll find yourself feeling stressed. All the traditional festivities are wonderfully heart-warming, but from tree trimming to gift wrapping they can be time- and energy-consuming in the extreme. We certainly know this at the North Pole! As Christmas approaches, we always find ourselves wishing there were more hours in the day.

Inevitably, other holiday demands sometimes cut down on the time you'd like to spend in the kitchen. Recognizing this, Lars set out to find a simple, nourishing dish that combines the elegance of festive dining with the ingredients that might somewhat offset the inevitable Christmas caloric indulgence, and as usual he succeeded quite brilliantly.

When you face a Christmas crunch, spare yourself and please your family by trying this wonderful salmon recipe, which requires less than thirty minutes to prepare. All of us at the North Pole love it—salmon is an especially tasty fish—and I personally enjoy the capers it contains. Discriminating diners have been enjoying these small buds for roughly five thousand years. We know so because they are mentioned in the Gilgamesh epic, perhaps the earliest known written story, which was discovered on Sumerian clay tablets dating from about 2700 B.C.

Poaching—preparing foods by placing them in simmering water—is one of the most ancient cooking techniques. There are poaching recipes in the very earliest cookbooks, which appeared in the first century A.D. Poached salmon almost certainly originated along North American shores; we know that Indian tribes often enjoyed this delectable dish. My dear friend Ben Franklin enjoys reminding us that America's founding fathers dined on poached salmon during the Independence Day celebrations of 1776. (Rumor had it that it was on the menu in deference to George Washington's false teeth; the soft texture of the dish made it easy for him to chew. Even if it's only a myth, it's a charming one!)

𝓛𝓪𝓻𝓪 𝓢𝓪𝔂𝓼: *"Fresh fish prepared simply and elegantly is always a special treat, even here at the North Pole. I often ask Santa to take the sleigh to Alaska and pick up some fresh salmon. He never minds running errands if food is involved. We much prefer wild salmon for its heartier taste, but farm-raised salmon is more than acceptable if that's what's available to you.*

"Many salmon recipes include complicated sauces. I suggest you try this dish all on its own. Though wine is among the ingredients, its alcohol content is cooked off, so this is a main course suitable for all ages and 'fancy' enough for holiday dining. Poaching in wine and topping with chives and capers enhances the flavor of the salmon without overwhelming it. Everyone will love this healthy, easy-to-prepare dish!"

2-lb. salmon fillet, cut into 4 to 6 pieces

2 cups dry white wine (Chardonnay or Pinot Blanc works
   especially well)

coarsely ground pepper (Use a pepper grinder for the best results.)

2 tsp. chopped fresh chives

2 tbsp. capers, drained and rinsed

1. Rinse the salmon fillet in cold water, then pat dry with paper towels. Cut the fillet crosswise into 4 to 6 pieces; set aside.

2. Pour the wine into a nonstick sauté pan. Arrange the salmon pieces in a single layer. Grind 1 tbsp. pepper over the salmon, then sprinkle with the chives. Cover the sauté pan snugly and place over low heat. Monitor carefully to make sure the wine barely simmers but doesn't quite boil. When you lift the cover, there should be only a moderate cloud of escaping steam.

3. About 5 minutes after the wine has begun to steam, the salmon should start to flake slightly. At this point, spoon the capers over the fish, replace the lid, and poach for 3 more minutes. When done, the fish should flake easily when prodded with a fork. Using a wide slotted spatula, transfer the fillets to warm dinner plates.

Bulgogi (Fire Meat)

From Korea

PREPARE: *30 minutes* • COOK: *5 minutes*
SERVES: *4 to 6*

Sung Dan Juk Ha! I've just wished you "Merry Christmas" in Korean! Our favorite holiday has been celebrated there for centuries, since about one in every four South Koreans is Christian. During the festive season, Koreans exchange Christmas cards, sing carols, decorate trees, have dinner parties for family and friends, and remind their children to go to bed early on December 24 so "Santa Grandfather" can come to leave them presents. On Christmas Day, families return home after church services to enjoy a Christmas feast. One course is often *bulgogi,* which is also known as *bul-kogi* or *bulgaki.* By any name, this is absolutely delectable barbecued beef.

4 tbsp. sesame seeds

2 tbsp. sugar

1 tbsp. sesame or vegetable oil

2 tbsp. soy sauce

1 green onion, chopped

1 clove garlic, finely chopped

1 tbsp. all-purpose flour

pinch of freshly ground black pepper

1 tbsp. sherry or beef broth

1 lb. lean beefsteak (round, sirloin, rib, or flank)

1. In a small dry skillet, slowly toast the sesame seeds over low heat, stirring occasionally, until brown. With a mortar and pestle grind the toasted seeds to a fine dust.
2. Combine the ground sesame seeds with all the remaining ingredients except the beef in a large bowl and mix thoroughly; set aside.

3. Slice the steak very thinly, cutting diagonally across the grain of the meat from top to bottom. This should result in slices about 1 1/2 inches long. Don't try to make the slices too thick or too long; you want lots of small, tasty bites of meat. Add the meat to the marinade and stir until all the slices are coated. Let stand at room temperature for at least 20 minutes; 30 minutes is even better.

4. Grill the meat over charcoal or under your oven broiler no more than 1 minute per side, until browned.

5. Serve hot, perhaps with rice and salad.

6. This main course is relatively inexpensive, quick to prepare, and a delightful holiday surprise for your dinner guests. Wish them *"Sung Dan Juk Ha"* before they're allowed to dig in!

Lars's Favorite Christmas Kebabs

From ancient Lycia (modern Turkey)

PREPARE: *20 minutes plus at least 2 hours for marinating*
COOK: *15 minutes* • SERVES: *6 to 8 (2 kebabs per person)*

S hish kebabs are dear to my heart as well as to my stomach. That's because this dish originates from my home country of Lycia, now known as Turkey. It was a favorite meal of my childhood: *sis* means "skewer" and *kebab* means "roast meat." There was no easier—or, to me, tastier—meal to prepare than skewered chunks of meat roasted over an open fire. Throughout the ages and around the world, people obviously agreed!

As you may recall from the Foreword, before joining us at the North Pole, Lars was a special friend to the children at a St. Paul, Minnesota, orphanage. Besides training many of them to become skilled, creative chefs in their own right, he annually presided over the preparation of a gala Christmas dinner for all the boys and girls there. Lars's yearly challenge was to come up with mouthwatering entrées on December 25 that didn't drain the facility's constantly strained food budget. And, of course, orphanage staffers aren't the only ones who feel a financial pinch during the holiday season; from purchasing Christmas trees to paying winter heating bills, it can be an expensive time of year.

One Christmas, Lars created a meal that combined every desirable holiday menu element. It looked wonderful, replete with traditional Christmas colors that lended themselves to spectacular plating and presentation. The ingredients weren't costly, and a little of each went a long way toward satisfying ravenous young appetites. It was fun to fix and easy, too; children of every age were able to help and simultaneously burn off some of their frantic Christmas energy. Above all, this dish tasted superb. Everyone loved it.

We especially recommend Lars's Favorite Christmas Kebabs to anyone who has been asked to bring a dish to a holiday party. You'll spend the evening being thanked by one and all.

Lars Says: *"Though there are some specific ingredients suggested in the recipe that follows, you can really mix and match to suit yourself and your budget. Shrimp, for instance, are lovely, but you can do fine without them. Some of my friends include bacon, and others don't. It's not mandatory to use red and green peppers; I just happen to love those holiday colors. Citrus juice in the marinade is crucial, but only a few specific juices are necessary. For the others, use what's on hand or on sale at your favorite grocery store.*

"Don't forget: If you use wooden skewers, soak them in water before cooking. Otherwise, they may catch fire, and you'll end up with charcoal kebabs!

"If you live in a warm climate, prepare these kebabs on a barbecue grill or hibachi. Should there be snow on the ground, underneath an oven broiler will do just fine."

1 lb. medium shrimp, peeled and deveined

1 lb. boneless, skinless chicken breast, cut into 1-inch cubes

¹/₂ lb. bacon, cut into 1¹/₂-inch pieces

THE MARINADE:

6 cups pineapple juice

juice of 2 lemons

juice of 2 limes

juice of 2 oranges

juice from whatever other citrus fruit you like

3 tbsp. brown sugar

1 tbsp. cayenne pepper

¹/₂ tsp. salt

THE KEBABS:

¹/₂ onion, cut into 1-inch chunks

1 large red bell pepper, cut into 1-inch chunks

1 large green bell pepper, cut into 1-inch chunks

8 ozs. pineapple chunks, drained if using canned

12 to 16 wooden or metal skewers

1. To marinate the shrimp and chicken: Place the shrimp in one resealable freezer bag and the chicken in another. To *each* bag, add 3 cups pineapple juice; the juice of 1 lemon, 1 lime, and 1 orange (plus additional citrus juices if you choose to use them); 1¹/₂ tbsp. of the brown sugar; ¹/₂ tbsp. of the cayenne; and ¹/₄ tsp. of the salt.

Seal each bag and gently shake to mix the marinade ingredients and thoroughly coat the shrimp and chicken. Set aside to marinate at room temperature for a minimum of 2 hours. You can certainly let them stay in the marinade overnight; just pop the bags into your refrigerator.

2. When you're ready to cook the kebabs, drain the shrimp and chicken well.

3. For the best flavor, and most attractive presentation, skewer the shrimp, chicken, onion, red and green pepper, and pineapple chunks in alternating order. For extra flavor, wrap each shrimp and chicken cube in bacon. Place the skewers on a grill rack or under an oven broiler, turning them occasionally, for 7 to 10 minutes, until the shrimp and chicken are completely cooked. Allow to cool for 2 minutes and serve.

"Feliz Navidad" Shrimp Enchiladas

From Mexico

PREPARE: *25 minutes* • COOK: *12 minutes*
SERVES: *4 (2 enchiladas per person)*

Christmas in Mexico combines all the best holiday traditions. There is great store set in worship. No one seems to forget that December 25 is, above all, a day to celebrate the birth of Christ. Most Mexican families attend Mass on Christmas Eve, and many return to church for Christmas morning services. These religious observances, however, do not preclude secular activities. There are innumerable Christmas parties, lots of strolling through streets singing carols, and plenty of nights when families gather together for bountiful holiday meals.

When people think of Mexican food, too many imagine simple enchiladas, tamales, and tacos, which are, of course, tasty in their own right, but there are many more interesting variations of these basic recipes, and here at the North Pole we are always thrilled when Lars emerges from the kitchen to serve one of them. Our special favorite during the holiday season is an entrée Lars has named *"Feliz Navidad"* Shrimp Enchiladas, a dish that annually comes very close to persuading us to move our toy-making operations from the North Pole to South of the Border.

6 fresh tomatillos, husked

1 cup chopped fresh cilantro

2 serrano peppers, slit lengthwise and seeded,
    if desired

2 jalapeño peppers, slit lengthwise and seeded,
    if desired

2 cloves garlic

1 lime, halved

2 tbsp. butter

1 tbsp. chili powder

1 tbsp. ground cumin

32 medium shrimp

8 flour tortillas

1/2 lb. white queso (cheese), finely grated

1. Preheat your oven to 325° F. Lightly grease a 13 by 9–inch baking pan; set aside.

2. Prepare the sauce: In a medium saucepan, boil the tomatillos until they just soften and their skins crack; drain.

3. Combine the tomatillos, cilantro, both types of pepper, garlic, and the juice from $1/2$ lime in a blender and puree until the mixture is slightly frothy and everything is thoroughly mixed. Transfer the mixture to a small saucepan and bring to a boil. Reduce the heat to low and simmer for several minutes, until the sauce thickens; set aside.

4. Melt the butter in a frying pan over medium heat. Add the juice of the remaining $1/2$ lime, the chili powder, and the cumin. Increase the heat to high, add the shrimp, and *quickly* sauté, turning the shrimp several times, until evenly coated and cooked through. This should take no longer than 2 minutes; you don't want to overcook the shrimp. Remove the pan from the heat. Using a slotted spoon, transfer the shrimp to a bowl.

5. Place 4 shrimp in each flat open tortilla, drizzle with a little of the sauce from the frying pan, then top with some of the *queso*. Roll up the tortillas, and place them in the prepared baking pan as snugly together as possible. You don't want them to unroll during cooking. Pour the remaining sauce evenly over the enchiladas and bake for 10 to 12 minutes, or just until the cheese has melted and the shrimp are heated through. Remove the pan from oven and let the enchiladas stand for 3 to 5 minutes before serving. *¡Feliz Navidad!*

Layla's Festive Lamb Stew

From ancient Lycia (modern Turkey)

❧

PREPARE: *30 minutes* • COOK: *2 ½ hours* • SERVES: *6 to 8*

Lars is a very thoughtful fellow, and sees to it that our North Pole holiday season dinners include plenty of dishes that were childhood favorites. We have different backgrounds and come from different times but we all share a love for tasty food. Among our favorite Christmastime dishes is a hearty lamb stew that my dear wife Layla's aunt originally showed her how to prepare nearly seventeen centuries ago. Layla, in turn, taught the recipe to Lars, who has added some modern touches with ingredients that weren't available when Layla was a child.

Layla was, in fact, born in A.D. 377 in a place then called Lycia and now known as Turkey. I'd been born ninety-seven years earlier in the same country. Layla hailed from a small farming community where people ate the grains, vegetables, and fruit they grew and the lambs and sheep they raised. As Christian families, they celebrated Christ's birth with prayer and feasting, though the feasts were necessarily modest. No one could, for instance, prepare roast beef because they had no cows. Any meat, in fact, was a rare treat. But celebrating the arrival of Baby Jesus was the most supremely joyous event of each year, and so lamb or mutton would be part of the holiday menu.

Poor families couldn't afford great quantities of meat, so it was natural for Lycians to cook stews for their special festive meals, adding lamb to pots brimming with locally available root vegetables and spices. So when you prepare this stew, please realize you are eating the very same dish that Santa and Mrs. Claus enjoyed during their own childhoods, long before they embarked on their gift-giving mission! And if, perhaps, I'm flying my sleigh nearby and smell the savory aroma unique to what we at the North Pole now call Layla's Festive Lamb Stew, I'll tether my reindeer on the lawn while I drop in to share your dinner.

Lara Says: *"One bite, and you'll understand why Layla still considers this her favorite dish ever. Students of food history will recognize that some of the ingredients I've added to the original recipe—potatoes, for instance (more on potatoes in the next section of this book), mushroom broth (available in handy boxes in many stores), and tomato paste—weren't available in Layla's childhood. These items enhance the flavor of the stew without overwhelming its original robust taste."*

❅

2 tbsp. olive oil
1 tbsp. butter
2 cloves garlic, minced
2 tbsp. fresh rosemary
1 lb. lamb sirloin, cut into bite-size pieces
2 cups dry red wine
6 cups mushroom broth
5 medium potatoes, peeled and chopped
½ lb. mushrooms, caps and stems, chopped

1 large tomato, coarsely chopped
1/2 large onion, chopped
3 stalks celery, chopped
1 tbsp. chopped fresh parsley
1 tbsp. fresh thyme
2 bay leaves
salt and freshly ground pepper to taste
2 (6-oz.) cans tomato paste

1. Heat the oil and butter in a large pot over medium heat. Add the garlic and rosemary and cook until the garlic has softened but hasn't browned. Add the lamb and cook, stirring occasionally, several minutes, until the lamb is completely browned. Pour in 1 cup of the red wine and continue to cook, scraping up the browned bits that have stuck to the bottom of the pan, until the wine is hot but not boiling. (This ensures especially tender lamb; nothing spoils a good stew more than tough, chewy meat!)

2. Add the broth, all the vegetables, all the remaining seasonings, and the remaining 1 cup wine. Reduce the heat to low, and let everything gently simmer until heated through.

3. Add the tomato paste, stirring with a wooden spoon until completely blended, and let the stew simmer, stirring occasionally, for at least 2 hours, until it has thickened, the lamb is tender, and the vegetables are completely cooked.

4. Turn off the heat and let the stew rest for about 10 minutes before serving. This will be one of the richest, most satisfying stews you've ever tasted and the perfect dish for a cold December night.

Lechón Asado (Pork Roast)

From Cuba

PREPARE: *35 minutes (You begin the night before!)* • COOK: *3 hours*

SERVES: *8 to 10*

I have many Cuban friends, one of whom, a lovely woman named Guille (pronounced "GHEE-yay"), has taught Lars a recipe for pork roast that is simply astounding. You must try it yourself. The ingredients are readily found in Cuban grocery stores.

Nowadays, beef is difficult to come by in Cuba. You would have to wait a very long time for a chance at turkey there. But pork is generally available, and at Christmastime Guille and other holiday-loving Cubans find novel ways to prepare this meat. In this recipe the *mojo,* or marinade, is crucial.

Of course, the Cuban government would prefer that its citizens not celebrate Christmas at all. So when you sit down to enjoy this marvelous meal, please pause for a moment to offer silent thanks in honor of those men, women, and children whose devotion to Christmas is stronger than their fear of government reprisals for observing the holiday. Someday, I pray, we'll live in a world where all people are free to express their beliefs without repression. Until then, enjoy this pork roast in honor of our Christmas-loving friends in Cuba!

❄

1 whole head of garlic (all the cloves), peeled and diced

1 tbsp. chopped fresh oregano

1 tbsp. ground cumin

$1/2$ tbsp. freshly ground black pepper

1 tsp. salt

$1/4$ cup white vinegar

$1/2$ cup white cooking wine

$1/2$ cup red cooking wine

1 center-cut pork loin filet (about 2 lbs.)

$1/2$ cup olive oil

1. Prepare the *mojo* (marinade): In a small container with a tight-fitting lid, combine the garlic, oregano, cumin, pepper, salt, vinegar, and white and red wine, and stir with a fork until blended. Cover and refrigerate until ready to use.

2. Prepare the roast: On the night before you intend to serve the meal, place the pork loin in a large container. Spoon the *mojo* over the pork until the pork is thoroughly coated. Unlike some other dishes with marinades, you don't need to immerse the whole roast with the spicy liquid. Cover the pork and refrigerate overnight.

3. Three hours before you want to serve the roast, cover the bottom of a Dutch oven with the oil and heat over medium-high heat until the oil is very hot. Remove the pork from the marinade and pat dry with paper towels. Add the pork to the hot oil and brown on all sides. Add the marinade and bring to a boil. Reduce the heat, cover, and simmer for 2 hours and 15 minutes.

4. Forty-five minutes before serving, remove the pork from the pot. Using a sharp knife, make deep cuts in the meat. This will allow the *mojo* to completely infuse the pork. Then return the pork to the pot, and continue to braise the meat.

5. Guille likes to serve her Christmas Cuban pork with a hearty side of black beans and rice (that recipe comes in the next section). We hope you'll give this dish a try; it will likely become one of your favorite holiday meals, too.

Attila's Old Country Chicken and Dumplings with Sauerkraut

From Germany

PREPARE: *20 minutes* • COOK: *2 1/2 hours* • SERVES: *4*

We mustn't forget that in many parts of the Christmas-celebrating world, chicken is the most widely available, economically priced meat. Accordingly, it serves as the basis for many delicious Christmas dinners, one of the most traditional of which, chicken and dumplings, is a dish that's considerably more robust than many of us usually realize. But Lars knows better, because Attila the Hun has taught him well.

Attila, of course, is known primarily as a warrior rather than a gastronome. But in the course of his long life—which, since our original meeting in A.D. 453, has actually been devoted to gift giving rather than fighting—he's certainly learned a thing or two about food and old-fashioned ways of preparing hearty dishes.

In Attila's case, because he originally hails from Asia Minor and then later from what became known as Europe, his favorite recipes often involve that most misunderstood of tangy ingredients: sauerkraut. Without refrigeration, people in Attila's day and beyond, couldn't successfully store food for any great length of time. Fermenting was one of the very earliest methods people used to prepare and preserve food. Sauerkraut, which is fermented cabbage, was one of the first foods mankind learned to treat in such a way that it could be saved for subsequent meals.

We think the Manchurians developed the process about two thousand years ago. Certainly the Chinese adopted the recipe. European families learned the secrets of sauerkraut during times of invasion from the East, and by the time great ships explored the world's oceans for the first time, crews ate a steady diet of sauerkraut because it would keep almost indefinitely and helped prevent scurvy (sauerkraut has a high vitamin C content and is very good for you). Eventually English crews brought along limes instead, while Germanic sailors remained sauerkraut loyalists. This explains the slang names of "limeys" for Englishmen and "krauts" for Germans.

Don't worry; we're not going to suggest that you ferment your own sauerkraut for Attila's favorite holiday dish; it's readily available in stores. But this lovely, traditional recipe will certainly grace your table and please your taste buds anytime during the Christmas season.

Lars Says: *"I absolutely hated sauerkraut when I was a little boy, but it's one of those unique tastes that eventually grows on you. So, even if your children beg you, don't eliminate sauerkraut from this recipe. It will, in fact, provide just that little extra kick necessary to elevate a supposedly familiar dish from mundane to memorable. Isn't that what holiday meals are supposed to be about?"*

THE CHICKEN:

1 (1½-lb.) chicken, cut into pieces
2 (14-oz.) cans chicken broth
1 small onion, chopped
½ cup chopped celery
2 bay leaves
2 cups sauerkraut
water
1 tsp. salt

THE DUMPLINGS:

1½ cups all-purpose flour
1 tsp. salt
4 tsp. baking powder
1 egg
1 tbsp. vegetable oil
⅔ cup whole milk

1. Place the chicken in a large pot or Dutch oven. Add the broth, onion, celery, and bay leaves. Add the sauerkraut and enough water to cover everything and bring to a boil over high heat. Cover, reduce the heat, and simmer, stirring occasionally and adding just enough water to keep the chicken pieces covered, for 2½ hours.
2. About 20 minutes before the chicken is ready, it's time to prepare the dumplings. *Slowly* increase the heat under the pot so the liquid in it will just reach the boiling point. Then combine the flour, salt, and baking powder in a medium bowl. Beat

the egg, vegetable oil, and milk in a small bowl until blended. Add the liquid mixture to the flour mixture and stir just until completely blended. Be careful not to overmix.

3. Drop the dumpling batter, 1 teaspoonful at a time, into the boiling liquid in the pot. Reduce the heat slightly (you want a very *gentle* boil), cover, and cook for 8 to 10 minutes, or until done. If you're not sure whether the dumplings are ready, take one out and push a wooden toothpick into it. If the toothpick pulls out clean, the dumplings are ready. Serve immediately.

Side Dishes

I t's not always the main course that makes a meal memorable. Here at the North Pole, some of our merriest feasts derive much of their pleasure from accompanying dishes, many of which reflect holiday customs from around the world. Lars is a master of these; he believes succulent "sides" lend themselves to overall meal excellence in the same way colored lights and tinsel enhance the beauty of a Christmas tree.

As you go about your holiday activities, you may find it quite pleasant to attempt some of the recipes that follow in this section. They vary in complexity of preparation and cooking difficulty, but it would be impossible to find a family or circle of friends who wouldn't enjoy tucking into any of them. Lars has included some tips on which side dishes go best with what main courses.

These recipes also will come in handy if you're invited to a gathering whose guests are asked to bring a side dish to complement the host's main course; any one of these would be perfect. You will even be able to offer a bit of appropriate Christmas history for each. That's part of the fun of international Christmas cooking: You can enjoy delicious meals while extending the holiday traditions of individual cultures.

Helena Zurek's *Kutya* (Wheat Porridge)

From Poland

PREPARE: *5 minutes* • COOK: *20 minutes* • SERVES: *8 to 10*
Goes well with any fish dish.

On Christmas Eve in Poland, families gather outside at twilight to anxiously look for the Gwiazdka, or "First Star of the Night," which symbolizes the Star of Bethlehem, the star that appeared on the night Jesus was born. Christmas Day is a time for everyone to gather together for *wigilia,* a memorable multicourse meal that follows a very strict ceremony. One chair at the table is always left vacant for the Christ Child or the Holy Spirit. Often, bits of hay are scattered on the white tablecloth, so everyone will remember that Jesus was born as a poor baby in a manger. And the meal always includes hearty portions of a delicious pudding called *kutya* whose ingredients represent aspects of life and tradition: walnuts for the hope of better times, poppy seeds for peace, and honey for the sweetness that is always possible in life. Our good friend Helena Zurek generously shared this recipe with Lars.

2 cups warm, cooked whole- or cracked-wheat berries
1 cup coarsely chopped walnuts
1/2 cup honey
2 tbsp. poppy seeds

1. Cook the wheat berries as directed on the package label.
2. In a medium mixing bowl, combine the walnuts, honey, and the cooked berries. Stir until blended and transfer to a serving bowl. Sprinkle with the poppy seeds and serve.
3. At the end of the meal the *kutya* is brought to the table and each person is given a spoon. The oldest guest or family member takes a spoonful, but before eating it, he or she wishes everyone present a long, happy life. Then the *kutya* is passed to everyone else in descending order of age, with each one taking a spoonful and offering an appropriate holiday wish. After everyone has had his or her turn, the remaining *kutya* is portioned out and enjoyed.

Kissel (Cranberry Puree)

From Russia

PREPARE: *5 minutes* • COOK: *10 minutes* • SERVES: *12*
Goes well with holiday goose or turkey.

Until the revolution of 1917, perhaps no country celebrated Christmas more than Russia. Saint Nicholas brought his gifts on December 6, and on January 7 church bells rang and holiday carols echoed along every street. (Russian Orthodox Catholics follow their own calendar, and so Christmas there falls on January 7 rather than December 25.) But in 1917 the Communist government banned such celebrations and, in fact, religious festivities of any sort.

This didn't prevent true believers from quietly enjoying private celebrations. Since Saint Nicholas was illegal, children were taught to look forward to holiday season visits from Ded Moroz, or Grandfather Frost. I was delighted to oblige them by using that new name, which certainly was charming enough.

But things changed again in Russia, and in 1992, seventy-five years after it was banned, the Christmas holiday was restored to the people. Christmas Day is once again widely celebrated with worship, carols, gifts, and fine food!

Kutya is a traditional holiday dish in Russia as well as in Poland, but my Russian friends also like to mark the Christmas season by serving *kissel,* an easy-to-prepare cranberry dish that will satisfy the heartiest appetites. I know I'm always pleased each time

Lars prepares this tasty side dish in the North Pole kitchen. Welcome to Christmas in Russia!

❄

1 lb. fresh (not frozen) cranberries
2 1/2 cups water
1/4 cup cornstarch
1/2 cup sugar
whipped cream for garnish (optional)

1. Combine the cranberries and 2 cups of the water in a medium saucepan and bring to a boil over high heat. Cook, stirring frequently, for about 5 minutes, until the berries are soft. Remove from the heat and allow the berries to cool slightly, until warm rather than hot.

2. Transfer the warm mixture to a blender or food processor with the metal blade attached and puree until smooth. Then return the cranberry puree to the saucepan.

3. Stir the cornstarch and the remaining 1/2 cup water in a small bowl until smooth.

Add the cornstarch mixture and the sugar to the cranberry puree and stir until well blended. Cook over medium heat, stirring frequently, for about 5 minutes, until the puree thickens.

4. You may serve *kissel* either warm or chilled. In either case, pour the mixture into individual serving bowls, and top with dollops of whipped cream, if you wish.

Coat of Arms (Spicy Peas)

From Jamaica

PREPARE: *15 minutes* • COOK: *35 minutes* • SERVES: *4 to 6*
Goes well with chicken, beef, or pork.

Y ou know it's Christmastime in Jamaica when you experience your first Jonkanoo. This festive event finds whole communities dancing down the streets singing carols and demonstrating the joy they feel during the holiday season. While some Jonkanoos are staged in major Jamaican cities, they're most common in the small country villages.

And the carols being sung? Why, the same ones you and your family probably sing, from "Silent Night" to "Jingle Bells"! These otherwise familiar tunes, however, are rendered in Jamaica with an infectious reggae beat. You must visit Jamaica sometime during the holidays to hear them for yourself; they're simply enchanting.

That's also true of Jamaica's special holiday meals. One of the tastiest is a spicy side dish that would perfectly complement almost any entrée. And I do mean *spicy*; there's nothing bland about this Jamaican Christmas treat.

2 (16-oz.) cans coconut milk (not cream of coconut)
2 cups uncooked rice
1 onion, finely chopped
1 clove garlic, finely chopped
2 (16-oz.) cans black-eyed peas, drained and rinsed
hot red pepper sauce
salt and freshly ground pepper

1. Combine the coconut milk, rice, onion, and garlic in a medium saucepan and bring to a boil over high heat, stirring constantly. Reduce the heat to low, cover, and simmer gently for about 30 minutes, or until all the liquid has been absorbed.
2. Add the peas, hot sauce (not *too* much the first time you try making this!), and salt and pepper to taste. Cover and cook over low heat for another 5 minutes. Serve immediately.

Christmas *Fufu* (Mashed Yams)

From Ghana

PREPARE: *10 minutes* • COOK: *45 minutes* • SERVES: *6*
Goes well with Doro Wat *(page 98), the spicy Ethiopian chicken stew.*
It's also good with any poultry dish.

In Ghana, Christmas revelers decorate mango or guava trees rather than pine. Families gather together to celebrate the holidays and invite total strangers to join them. In every sense, Christmas is a communal festival. It is impossible for Ghanians to pass anyone without calling out a heartfelt "*Afishapa,*" which combines best wishes for a Merry Christmas and a Happy New Year.

As Father Christmas, I'm expected to arrive on Christmas Eve and to leave gifts of cookies and chocolate for all the children, who often don't actually receive my gifts until after they've attended church on Christmas Day. No one in Ghana ever seems to forget that the primary purpose of the holiday is to celebrate the birth of Jesus.

And, as in every Christmas-loving country, natives of Ghana like to mark the Christmas season with tasty meals. Often, their budgets are limited, and so they have learned to turn staples of their ordinary diets into something particularly lip-smacking during the holidays. *Fufu* is a good example.

1 1/2 lbs. yams
1 tsp. ground nutmeg
salt and freshly ground pepper

1. Wash the yams thoroughly and pat dry with paper towels; allow to stand for 5 minutes. Boil the yams for 30 minutes in a large pot with enough water to cover. Test with a fork for doneness. When fully cooked, remove from the heat and drain. Set aside to cool to room temperature, about 10 minutes.

2. When the yams are cool enough to handle, peel them and then cut them into small chunks. If using a potato masher, transfer the yams to a medium bowl. Or if using a food processor with the steel blade attached, process or mash into a thick, lump-free paste. Add the nutmeg and season with salt and pepper to taste. Stir until blended.

3. With wet, clean hands, shape the mixture into a rounded loaf or into golf ball–size spheres. Place on a serving plate. As in Ghana, each person should either pinch off some of the loaf or take one or two *fufu* balls. It's a communal dish, meant to symbolize sharing.

Ensalada Navideña
(Nativity Salad)

From Mexico

PREPARE: *1 1/2 hours* • SERVES: *8*
Goes well with anything; it's fruit salad!

How I look forward every year to my Christmas Eve visit to Mexico, where I'm known as Papá Noel! By the time I arrive, however, holiday festivities are already well under way. The excitement begins on December 16, the first of nine consecutive days for *posadas*, lovely processions through city and village streets.

Posada is the Spanish word for "inn," and the purpose of the parade is to reenact the efforts of Joseph and Mary to find a place to stay in Bethlehem. Each procession is led by children, often with one dressed as an angel and two more carrying figures of Mary and Joseph. They lead everyone to a house that has been designated in advance. Where the weary "expectant parents" knock on the door and ask for shelter, which is loudly denied. But when they explain that a baby is about to be born, they are invited inside. Then everyone enjoys snacks and drinks. What a wonderful tradition!

One of the favorite snacks is *Ensalada Navideña,* a very tasty salad that is beloved by adults and children equally. It takes some time to prepare, but the result is colorful and delicious. I promise that your family and friends will love it, and Santa Claus *never* breaks his word!

Lara Says: *"I urge you to use fresh rather than canned beets; this makes a considerable difference in taste. I know that using beets at all is unusual because they've somehow fallen out of favor with many modern cooks. Let's restore their popularity, starting with* Ensalada Navideña!*"*

THE SALAD:

2 large beets

3 whole oranges

3 bananas

½ jícama

1 (16-oz.) can pineapple chunks, drained

1 pomegranate

1 head iceberg lettuce

1 (12-oz.) package almonds

THE DRESSING:

3 tbsp. fresh lime juice

9 tbsp. vegetable oil

1½ tsp. brown sugar

dash of salt

1. Boil the beets *with skin on* until they are fully cooked, about 30 minutes. Drain and set aside to cool to room temperature. Then peel the beets and cut them into small cubes or chunks. Place the beets in a small bowl. Cover and refrigerate until chilled.

2. While the beets are boiling, peel the oranges, bananas, and jícama. Holding each piece of fruit over a large bowl, cut into small chunks, allowing the pieces to fall into the bowl. Add the pineapple. Cover and refrigerate until chilled.

3. Halve the pomegranate and, using a spoon, remove the seeds; set aside.

4. When you're ready to complete the salad, shred the lettuce. Place the shredded lettuce in a *large* salad bowl. Add the fruit and the beets and toss gently until evenly mixed. Sprinkle with the almonds and pomegranate seeds.

5. Combine all the dressing ingredients in a small bowl and whisk until blended. Drizzle the dressing over the salad and toss until evenly coated. *Feliz Navidad* from Papá Noel!

Moros y Cristianos
(Black Beans and Rice)

From Cuba

PREPARE: *25 minutes plus 24 hours for soaking* • COOK: *4 hours*
SERVES: *8*
Goes well with Lechón Asado *(page 125),* Hallacas *(page 93),*
or any meat dish.

There's nothing better than a hearty, hot meal on a cold winter's night, and this Cuban dish is perfect for satisfying appetites and delighting taste buds. You may want to serve it with the delectable Cuban pork roast described earlier. And all by itself, *Moros y Cristianos* (literally, Moors and Christians) is a holiday treat that even picky eaters love.

When celebrating the Christmas holidays, many Cuban families have little money to spend on food. Grocery store stock is also limited in variety, so the challenge is to blend familiar, affordable ingredients in special ways. So here we have staple items—black beans, rice, garlic, chicken broth—plus a few "extras" brought together in an especially flavorful way.

Lara Says: *"This recipe for* Moros y Cristianos *goes back to the 1500s, when Spanish troops drove off native Cuban tribes and populated much of the island with African slaves. Beans and rice were the basis of slave diets, which offered little in the way of variety, except during Christmastime, when garnishes were occasionally added.*

"So when you prepare and serve this dish, you're creating a holiday link that goes back at least five centuries. Please note that the black beans must be soaked overnight before you start cooking. If you skip this step, the beans will be hard as rocks, which, as you can imagine, would spoil everyone's enjoyment of them!

"When I serve Moros y Cristianos *at the North Pole, everyone wants seconds, and Santa has been known to ask for thirds. If Mrs. Claus isn't looking, we're glad to oblige him."*

1 lb. dried black beans

4 (14-oz.) cans chicken broth

$\frac{1}{4}$ cup plus 1 tsp. olive oil

1 large onion, chopped

3 green bell peppers, chopped

2 cloves garlic, minced

$\frac{1}{4}$ ham bone from cooked ham or

    1 packet ham-flavored concentrate

3 bay leaves

1$\frac{1}{2}$ tsp. salt

1 cup uncooked white rice
2 tsp. ground cumin
2 tsp. dried oregano
1 cup sour cream
¹/₂ cup chopped green onion for garnish

1. The night before serving, rinse the beans thoroughly. Then place them in a large pot with enough water to completely cover them. It's not a bad idea to fill up the pot to a level about 2 inches above the beans. Set aside to soak overnight.
2. About 4 hours before you plan to serve, rinse the beans again and place them in a large (at least 6-qt.) pot. Add 3 cans of the broth and place over medium heat. The beans should cook for at least 3 1/2 hours.
3. In a large skillet, heat 1/4 cup of the oil over medium-high heat. Add the onion and green peppers and sauté for 6 minutes. Then add the garlic and sauté for 1 more minute.
4. Add the onion mixture to the beans and stir until mixed. Then add the ham bone (or ham-flavored concentrate), bay leaves, and salt and bring to a boil. Reduce the heat, cover, and simmer gently, stirring every 20 minutes and adding broth as needed, until the beans are tender.
5. About 30 minutes before serving, cook the rice in water seasoned with the remaining 1 tsp. oil.
6. Ten minutes before serving, stir the cumin and oregano into the bean mixture.
7. Serve the beans over the rice with a hearty dollop of sour cream. Garnish each serving with the green onion.

Theodore Roosevelt's Pan-Fried Christmas Potatoes

From the U.S.A.

PREPARE: *15 minutes* • COOK: *20 minutes* • SERVES: *6*
Goes well with almost anything!

My good North Pole friend Theodore Roosevelt likes to remind us that, prior to his becoming president, he spent some years living the life of a cowboy in the Old West. And in common with most cowboys, Theodore did and does love celebrating Christmas. Out on the rolling plains or amid the towering hills, carol singing was always delightful. If any of the cowboys sang out of tune (and Theodore, bless him, has never to my knowledge quite managed to sing *in* tune), none of the cattle being herded or the wild horses being roped and tamed were ever known to complain.

Holiday meals, however, were more of a challenge, given the cowboys' limited larder and access to kitchens. But that never stopped Theodore from serving up special Christmas delights, which of necessity were simple to prepare and made with very basic ingredients. Potatoes were always handy; the cowboys would carry these in their saddlebags, along with tins of tomatoes, onions, and spices.

One Christmas, Theodore delighted his prairie companions with this mouthwatering potato dish, and even now he likes to serve it to us at the North Pole sometime each holiday season. Lars gladly gives up pride of place in the kitchen, and while eating we all gather 'round as Theodore tells of long-ago cowboy Christmases, when the strains of "Silent Night" and the aroma of gently frying potatoes filled the wild western skies.

Lars Says: *"People wrongly believe that anything beyond the most basic fare must be difficult to prepare. Theodore's holiday potato recipe should surprise those of you who share this mistaken notion. The simple potato has been a staple since about 200 B.C., going back to the ancient native peoples of Peru. In the 1500s, Spanish explorers who had contact with the Incas brought the first potatoes to Europe. Because they were filling and easy to grow, potatoes gradually became integral to European diets.*

"And we certainly love potatoes at the North Pole. The Incas didn't celebrate Christmas, but for many of their holidays they not only ate them but drank a strong beerlike brew that was squeezed from fermented potato. Fortunately, Theodore hasn't shared that recipe with us!"

2 1/2 cups vegetable oil

1 tbsp. fresh rosemary

2 tsp. fresh thyme

1/2 tsp. cayenne pepper

8 to 10 Yukon Gold potatoes, unpeeled and chopped

1 onion, chopped

1 tomato, chopped

4 green onions, chopped

2 cloves garlic, chopped
1 tbsp. butter
salt and freshly ground pepper

1. Combine the oil, rosemary, thyme, cayenne, and potato chunks in a medium saucepan over medium heat and cook for 10 minutes, until the oil is hot and the potatoes have begun to soften.
2. Add the onion, tomato, green onions, garlic, and butter and stir until thoroughly mixed. Cook for 10 more minutes. Remove the pan from the heat and add salt and pepper to taste. Drain off any excess oil and serve the potatoes piping hot.

Baked Mealies and Tomatoes
(Corn and Tomato Casserole)

From South Africa

PREPARE: *15 minutes* • COOK: *45 minutes* • SERVES: *8*
Goes well with roast beef or pork.
Vegetarians will find this a tasty main course.

South Africa draws its population from many cultures, so during the holiday season you may be wished a Merry Christmas in several languages: *Sinifisela Ukhisimusi Omuhle* in Zulu, for instance, or *Geseënde Kersfees* in Afrikaans. Children leap up from bed on Christmas morning to see what gifts Goosaleh has left for them, and families and friends gather at noon for Christmas lunch. Afterward, they exchange "Christmas boxes," usually parcels containing more delicious food.

Because December 25 is the middle of the South African summer, holiday meals are often lighter than those served in other parts of the world. That doesn't mean South Africa's Christmas specialties are any less delectable, however, and this recipe for Baked Mealies and Tomatoes is proof.

Perhaps you're already wondering what in the world "mealies" might be. That's the term South Africans use for corn kernels. All the ingredients in this dish are easy to find at your local supermarket.

2 cups corn kernels (fresh, canned, or frozen)

1 (16-oz.) can whole tomatoes, drained and chopped

2 eggs, lightly beaten

$^1/_4$ cup packed light brown sugar

1 cup 1-inch squares of lightly toasted white bread

salt and freshly ground pepper

$^1/_2$ cup bread crumbs

$^1/_4$ cup ($^1/_2$ stick) butter, melted

1. Preheat your oven to 325°F. Lightly grease a 1$^1/_2$-qt. casserole dish; set aside.
2. If using canned corn, drain. If using frozen corn, rinse under cold water to thaw.
3. In a large bowl, mix the corn, tomatoes, eggs, brown sugar, bread squares, and salt and pepper to taste. Transfer the mixture to the prepared casserole dish, spreading evenly.
4. Sprinkle with the bread crumbs and drizzle with the melted butter. Bake for about 45 minutes, until the bread crumb topping turns golden brown. Serve warm.

Lars's Traditional Cranberry Ambrosia

From the North Pole

PREPARE: *25 minutes (Prepare it the night before serving.)* • SERVES: *8*
Goes well with holiday turkey or ham.

Like many of you, we are admitted holiday traditionalists at the North Pole, and there are certain aspects of our Christmas celebration that remain exactly the same from year to year because we like it that way. When we all get back from our Christmas Eve gift giving tired and peckish, Lars greets us with mugs of hot chocolate and platters of homemade cookies, recipes for which will follow shortly. We like to sleep late on Christmas morning—after all, we had a late, hectic night! And when we sit down for our own Christmas dinner, cranberry salad must always be on the menu.

Cranberries are strongly associated with winter holidays, and America may claim much of the credit. Like blueberries, they are among the very few indigenous North American fruits. European settlers in the so-called New World soon learned that Indian tribes used cranberries as garnishes for many of their favorite foods, and the fruit gained instant popularity around the globe. The English called it "craneberry," believing its flowers looked like the heads of cranes.

Many people like cranberry dressing with their Thanksgiving turkey. Here at the North Pole we prefer a cranberry side dish that offers several different textures and tastes and is just a little sweet. (Cranberries are by nature very tart, and that's the wrong flavor for Christmas dining unless you're the Grinch.) So Lars, bless his culinary soul, set out to create a cranberry salad that would be easy to make, delightful to the eye, and delectable to the palate. As you'll see, he succeeded.

Lars Says: *"This is another recipe that's proven popular at office parties and potluck gatherings. Two critical elements include preparing it the night before—the Jell-O needs time to set—and not chopping the pecans and walnuts too fine—you want your friends to experience a satisfying crunch while consuming them. Too many people chop and chop until they are essentially using nut powder. We never make that mistake in the North Pole kitchens."*

1 (3-oz.) pkg. black cherry Jell-O
¹/₂ cup sugar
1 cup boiling water
1 cup fresh cranberries, coarsely ground in a food processor
1 cup mini marshmallows
1 cup finely chopped apples
¹/₄ cup chopped pecans
¹/₄ cup chopped walnuts

In a large bowl, combine the black cherry Jell-O, sugar, and boiling water, stirring until the gelatin has dissolved. Add the cranberries, marshmallows, apples, pecans, and walnuts and stir until mixed. Transfer to a 3-cup gelatin mold, cover, and chill until set. That's it!

Drinks

H oliday feasts are even more special when festive drinks are served. Around the world, a variety of tasty libations are associated with Christmas celebrations. At the North Pole we enjoy them all. In the case of those containing alcohol, we enjoy them in moderation.

The recipes that follow are for beverages that can be enjoyed by themselves without an accompanying meal. But whether you're eating or not when you sample these delicious drinks, you are certain to get into the Christmas spirit.

We begin with drink recipes that are appropriate for the entire family, then proceed to some liquid refreshments that are ideal for grown-up Christmas parties or for weary parents on Christmas Eve who would like to toast Santa with a nightcap and then slip off to bed. First on our list is that most traditional of Christmas drinks and, I gladly admit, the dearest to my heart—and taste buds!

Santa's Favorite Hot Chocolate

From Spain

PREPARE: *10 minutes* • BREW: *10 minutes* • SERVES: *4*

Who doesn't love chocolate in all its edible forms? A better question might be, who knows the real history of this wonderful confection?

Chocolate is extracted from the beans of the tropical cacao tree, and archaeologists searching old ruins have determined that the Mayas enjoyed chocolate drinks over twenty-five hundred years ago. They loved the beverage so much that many grew cacao trees in the gardens of their homes.

The Aztecs called this substance *chocolatl* and enjoyed it in both solid and liquid forms. *Chocolatl* was so much in demand that Aztec merchants often used it for currency.

Christopher Columbus brought cacao beans back to Spain during his first New World explorations, but it may have been explorer Hernán Cortés who discovered how to produce a drink sweet enough to enrapture members of the Spanish aristocracy by mixing sugarcane juice with liquefied cacao beans. For most of the 1500s, "hot chocolate" was a drink enjoyed almost exclusively in Spain. Explorers for other European nations had no idea what cacao/chocolate was. One legend has it that a British pirate who captured a Spanish barge laden with cacao beans burned the ship and its cargo because he mistook the beans for dried animal droppings.

But Spain couldn't keep its tasty secret forever, and in the 1600s virtually every country in Europe went chocolate-intensive, drinking it with glee. Eating chocolate as a snack came much later. The first modern chocolate bar wasn't produced until the 1840s, when an English manufacturer invented the treat that would satisfy everyone's sweet tooth for generations to come.

Still, at the North Pole we like to honor Spain's pioneering efforts in what would become modern chocolate consumption. So if you and your family traditionally enjoy cups of hot chocolate as part of your holiday merriment, I gladly recommend this recipe based on the traditional Spanish beverage.

ᴸᵃʳᵃ Says: *"Once again, you'll notice I've substituted a modern ingredient: They didn't have vanilla instant pudding back in medieval Spain. Even so, this is one of the richest chocolate drinks you'll ever enjoy. One delicious cup should be plenty for anyone, even the most devout lover of chocolate!"*

1 1/2 cups whole milk
4 ozs. dark cooking chocolate, chopped into small pieces
1 tbsp. vanilla instant pudding
whipped cream
pinch of freshly grated nutmeg (tinned ground nutmeg will do)

1. Warm ³/₄ cup of the milk in a nonstick saucepan over low heat. Add the chocolate and stir until all the chocolate has melted.

2. Mix the vanilla pudding and the remaining ³⁄₄ cup milk until blended. Add the pudding mixture to the warm chocolate mixture, stirring constantly, until the chocolate drink is thick. Do *not* allow to come to a boil. Remove from the heat and whisk until frothy. Serve in mugs topped with a dollop of whipped cream and a grating of nutmeg (or, if you prefer, grated dark chocolate).

Sparkling Ruby Punch

From Canada

PREPARE: *5 minutes* • SERVES: *8 (per half gallon)*

During Christmastime at the St. Paul orphanage, Lars recognized a need for a festive holiday drink that could be prepared quickly and inexpensively. His research brought his attention to Canada, where a particular beverage has become a special favorite at children's Christmas parties. Even adults find it delicious, and because so much fruit juice is included, the argument can even be made that it's a very healthy drink.

It's become our tradition at the North Pole to gather and enjoy a hearty drink of Canadian Sparkling Ruby Punch just before setting out to deliver our gifts all over the world. It tastes so clean and refreshing, your family will want it every Christmas from now on.

Lars Says: *"I think one of the reasons children like this drink so much is that it seems quite special and sophisticated, a grown-up beverage without any alcohol. The ingredients are readily available and inexpensive, so you can easily make a lot for little cost. For a special touch, try garnishing the glasses with thin slices of lemon. Cheers!"*

5 cups apple juice
5 cups cranberry juice
juice of 1 lemon
5 cups ginger ale

1. Combine the apple juice, cranberry juice, and lemon juice in a large bowl. Stir until well blended. Cover and refrigerate for at least 1 hour, until chilled.
2. Just before serving, add the ginger ale. That's it!

Salabat (Ginger Tea)

From the Philippines

PREPARE: *5 minutes* • BREW: *30 minutes* • SERVES: *6 to 8, depending on the number of requests for refills (Expect plenty of these!)*

The Christmas traditions of the Philippines are dear to my heart. The people there first begin singing Christmas carols in September, and they are so reluctant to conclude their holiday festivities that decorations are taken down only on Tatlong Hari, or Three Kings' Day, celebrated on the first Sunday of the New Year. It is very much a family time: Everyone attends church together, enjoys celebratory meals together, and, almost every day, gathers to drink cups of delicious *salabat*.

Simple to prepare, tasty to consume, *salabat* would provide an extra sparkle to anyone's holiday season. It rivals hot chocolate as the favorite holiday beverage at the North Pole and contains considerably fewer calories.

Lars Says: *"You can find fresh gingerroot in most supermarkets. It isn't very expensive. When following this recipe, make sure you crush the chopped gingerroot completely. This will allow the full release of ginger flavor in the tea."*

6 ozs. fresh gingerroot
8 cups boiling water
1 cup honey
hot water

1. Peel the gingerroot and cut it into 1-inch pieces. Using a rolling pin or kitchen mallet, crush the ginger.
2. In a medium saucepan, combine the crushed ginger, boiling water, and honey and bring to a boil, stirring over high heat. Reduce the heat and simmer, adding more boiling water as needed to maintain a 6-cup level, for 30 minutes. Remove from the heat and set aside to cool to room temperature.
3. Strain the cooled tea through a coffee filter. (This removes all the bits of ginger.) Transfer to a large jar or pitcher, cover, and refrigerate until ready to serve.
4. To serve, pour about ¼ cup of the ginger tea into each mug. Fill the mug by adding hot water. Stir and add a little more honey if extra sweetness is desired.

Holiday Eggnog

From England

PREPARE: *20 minutes* • CHILL: *1 hour* • SERVES: *10 (per half gallon)*

Eggnog is a drink with a long history. It has been enjoyed as a festive beverage in England for many centuries, but its form has changed considerably from the original.

My British friends and I originally liked posset, which consisted of curdled milk mixed with ale or sometimes wine. Milk was a rare treat for most people in England in times past; beer was a far more common beverage. Remember, there were no refrigerators then, and cows were mostly the property of the rich.

In the 1800s, posset gave way to a drink first known as an "egg flip." The egg flip was sweeter and sometimes was served without any alcohol. Its name was soon altered to "eggnog," which paid tribute to the old English nickname of "noggin" for a glass of strong beer.

Different cultures prepared eggnog in different ways, sometimes supplying their own names to the drink. Syllabub from the American South is a good example. Actually, *syllabub* is yet another name for an early form of eggnog, *sillie* being a term for "wine" and *bub* Old English slang for a drink that bubbles. Southerners simply grafted the term onto their special drink that combined sweet cream, fruit juice, and wine or liquor.

Modern eggnog always includes some traditional ingredients—eggs, certainly, and lots of sugar—and sometimes incorporates relatively new ones like ice cream. The recipe I'm sharing here is one anyone would love. The brandy is optional, and the drink itself is not quite as thick as the commercial eggnog available during the holidays at many grocery stores.

Lara Says: "Everyone should try making fresh eggnog. It's a fun process, and the results are delicious. I admit that some eggnog traditionalists will disagree with me about including ice cream, but once you sample it, you'll always want ice cream in your eggnog.

"There are always risks with consuming raw eggs. We suggest that children, pregnant women, and people with challenged immune systems skip this holiday drink.

"I want to stress that this or any other eggnog tastes wonderful with or without alcohol. If you do choose to include what some call 'spirits,' feel free to substitute rum, bourbon, or cognac for the brandy. Happy drinking!"

6 eggs, separated
8 tbsp. sugar
1 cup ($^1/_2$ pint) heavy or whipping cream
6$^1/_2$ cups whole milk
$^1/_4$ cup brandy or more (optional)
1 qt. vanilla ice cream
freshly grated nutmeg (optional)

1. In a large bowl, beat the egg yolks until smooth. Add 6 tbsp. of the sugar, the cream, 6 cups of the milk, and (if you're using it) the brandy and mix well. Cover and refrigerate for a minimum of 1 hour, until chilled.
2. Before serving, in a small bowl beat the egg whites until frothy. Then add the remaining 2 tbsp. sugar and $\frac{1}{2}$ cup milk and stir just until blended.
3. Remove the egg yolk mixture from the refrigerator. Add the egg white mixture and stir just until blended. Add the ice cream. It's your choice whether to leave the ice cream in one large block or to break it up into individual scoops. Sprinkle nutmeg on top (if desired) and serve, using a ladle to fill individual mugs. The ice cream will gradually melt in the mugs, adding a delectable consistency and underlying smooth flavor. You, your family, and friends will never settle for commercial eggnog again.

Glühwein ("Glow" Wine)

From Germany

PREPARE: *10 minutes* • BREW: *30 minutes* • SERVES: *12*

At the North Pole, German *Glühwein* (literally, "glow wine") offers welcome relief during the frantic days before the holidays when we work long and hard to build toys for children all over the world. Even my friends and I need a little time to relax from our labors, and when we do we count on Lars to appear with mugs of this delicious brew. The taste is hearty but not heavy. Small sips satisfy; there's no need to gulp. Accordingly, *Glühwein* lends itself perfectly to sitting and chatting with friends. It is by its nature a convivial, relaxing drink, just the thing for those moments in the Christmas season when a break from the hectic pace seems appropriate.

Lars Says: "Glühwein *is very much a drink of the German/Austrian region, and I discovered this recipe at Innsbruck, in the Alps. I would like to reiterate Santa's suggestion that this is something to sip rather than gulp; the warm, spicy mixture does include a significant amount of alcohol and has a kick, though you might not realize it at the time.*

"Some specialty food stores sell Glühfix, *little bags of spice that can be substituted for some of the ingredients listed here. The spice bags are fine, but I personally enjoy the few extra steps. Preparing* Glühwein *the old-fashioned way somehow seems to enhance the enjoyment of the drink itself."*

3 cups water
1 cup sugar
$\frac{1}{8}$ tsp. ground allspice
4 cinnamon sticks
8 whole cloves
2 oranges, sliced
1 lemon, sliced
2 (750-ml) bottles red wine
$\frac{1}{2}$ cup brandy

1. In a large saucepan, combine the water, sugar, allspice, cinnamon sticks, cloves, orange slices, and lemon slices and bring to a boil. Reduce the heat and simmer for 10 minutes. Remove from the heat and strain.
2. Return the strained liquid to the saucepan. Reduce the heat to warm; don't boil! Add the wine and brandy. Allow the mixture to steep for 10 minutes before serving.

Julglögg
(Christmas Mulled Wine)

From Finland

PREPARE: *10 minutes* • BREW: *1½ hours*
SERVES: *about 12*

No Scandinavian holiday gathering is complete without lots of *julglögg*, a potent brew that always combines alcohol, fruit, and spices—but not always the same ones. There are many variations, but you may be certain that some form of *julglögg* or another is being served in nearly every Scandinavian home during the Christmas season.

At the North Pole, we enjoy *julglögg* both for its own sake and in honor of the holiday traditions it represents. In Finland, for example, stores close at noon on December 24 because every shopkeeper knows that Finnish families are gathering in their homes to begin an extended celebration. No one leaves their Christmas shopping until the last minute! And exactly at noon, Finland proclaims Peace of Christmas, a signal for the first round of holiday dining and drinking to begin.

After a lengthy meal, most families visit the graves of their dear departed, so that these loved ones can, in a sense, share in the celebration. Because the sky is already dark, the processions are lit by handheld candles; it's a very moving sight indeed.

Afterward, children prepare for bed in hopes that Joulupukki, Father Christmas, will soon be arriving. In keeping with Finland's traditions, I carry my gifts in a basket rather than a sleigh. To Finnish boys and girls, my home is Korvatunturi, or Ear Mountain. In any event, gift giving in Finland involves a long, chilly trip!

And that is why Santa, like many grown-ups in Finland, likes to mark his Christmas Eve visit with a warming mug of *julglögg*. I recommend it to all who stay up late on that night making certain that the little ones will awaken Christmas morning to find just the right presents from Santa waiting for them under the tree.

Lars Says: *"If* Glühwein *is a folk song among holiday drinks, then* julglögg *is a symphony. Some of the same ingredients are involved, but the preparation of* julglögg *is more complicated, and the resulting taste is more complex. It's certainly a spectacular-looking as well as -tasting drink. I haven't met anyone yet who wasn't amazed by it.*

"My recipe calls for brandy. In Sweden, most recipes include aquavit instead. I like orange peel. Others prefer dried cherries. I encourage you, over the next few Christmases, to try your own variations. It's fun, and usually a little experimentation with the ingredients doesn't spoil the overall taste. No one has yet come up with the definitive combination of ingredients for julglögg; *perhaps you'll be the one to invent the recipe that everyone else agrees is perfect. But start with this one!"*

1 (1.5-liter) bottle dry red wine (cabernet or merlot)
¼ bottle port
3 to 4 cinnamon sticks (about 10 inches)
½ tbsp. cardamom seeds
2 dozen whole cloves
½ cup raisins
peel of 1 orange
1 cup blanched almonds
2 cups sugar
1 (12-oz.) bottle brandy

1. Combine red wine and port in a large stainless-steel pot. Add cinnamon, cardamom seeds, cloves, raisins, orange peel, and almonds. Warm over low heat, but don't boil; you don't want to burn off the alcohol!

2. In a separate pan, mix the sugar and half the bottle of brandy. Warm over low heat until the sugar has melted and you're left with a lovely golden syrup. Add the syrup to the spiced wine mixture, cover, and allow to mull for 1 hour.

3. Before serving, strain the wine to remove all solids. Then add the remainder of the brandy and heat through. Serve warm, and warn your guests that this is a holiday drink with a considerable wallop!

Desserts

More than with any other dishes, I believe that people associate Christmas with desserts. Holiday baking seems natural; from the time humans celebrated anything, they did so with meals including special treats, and what better treat can there be than a luscious dessert?

At the North Pole, desserts are Lars's specialty. In addition to the many that have been traditional for centuries in one Christmas-celebrating country or another, he has created a few himself. Like all of us, Lars believes in the *festiveness* of dessert. Who, after all, can feel glum while devouring melt-in-your-mouth cake or rich pudding? There's a reason children love to leave me cookies on Christmas Eve: They know, as I do, that cookies are *joyful* food.

You'll notice that most of the recipes that follow are not for calorie counters. We recognize and appreciate the fact that for most of the year "eating healthy" is wise. But all of us at the North Pole also suspect that, come Christmastime, everyone likes to treat him-or herself to a little caloric self-indulgence.

Any of these desserts will please your family or guests at a holiday party, and most are relatively simple to prepare. In every case, make sure the chef also has the opportunity to enjoy the results of his or her labor. Even Lars wants second helpings of all these sweet delights!

We'll begin with a dish Lars originally concocted for his beloved orphans. At the time, he didn't realize that a key ingredient would delightfully remind me of my own childhood.

Nonna's Patara Pudding

From the North Pole

PREPARE: *45 minutes plus a minimum of 6 hours for chilling*
COOK: *20 minutes* • SERVES: *12*

I was born in A.D. 280 in the Lycian town of Patara, where my father, Epiphaneos, and mother, Nonna, operated a small inn. They named me Nicholas, which means "Victorious," because they were in their fifties when I was born, and no one believed they could have a baby.

My parents passed away when I was nine, and for the rest of my childhood I was raised by local priests, but I remember my parents well, even though I haven't seen them for the better part of eighteen centuries. The holidays are the perfect time to reflect on those we've known and loved. No one is really gone forever as long as someone is left to remember them fondly.

One of my best memories concerns my mother's cooking. She was like Lars in that she had a knack for combining otherwise ordinary ingredients in amazing, delectable ways. Whenever she prepared a special dessert for me, it always included cherries, which originated in the Lycian (later Turkish) town of Cerasus, not far from where I lived.

Cherries are the most delightful fruit, sweet if prepared in some ways and slightly sour in others. Mother would stew cherries in delightful broths or cook them in pastries. I loved all of her creations. So imagine my delight when Lars astounded us in his first days at the

North Pole with a pudding that included cherries among other delicious ingredients. To honor my mother, he named the pudding after her, and because of that, if for no other reason, it became my favorite Christmas dessert. But I also love it because it tastes so good. You and your friends will enjoy it, too.

 *Lars Says: "I originally came up with this recipe so all the St. Paul orphans could enjoy a filling, tasty dessert as part of their Christmas dinner. The ingredients of Nonna's Patara Pudding aren't very expensive, and there's plenty of the dessert to go around, which makes it perfect for serving at holiday parties where lots of people need hearty helpings.*

"I've found that children love this pudding because it looks so odd: lumpy and full of different textures. That's part of the charm. When you see it before you first taste it, you don't think it will be very good. Moments later, you're begging for seconds.

"Remember: You must prepare this dessert the night before you intend to serve it."

❄

6 eggs
1½ cups sugar
2 cups (1 pt.) milk
1 (12-oz.) box vanilla wafers
1 (16-oz.) jar maraschino cherries
2 small (7-g.) envelopes gelatin
1 cup chopped nuts (Pick your favorite; pecans or walnuts are best.)

2 tsp. vanilla extract
1 cup heavy or whipping cream

1. Carefully separate the eggs, the whites into a large mixing bowl and set aside. Put the yolks in a large saucepan or stockpot.
2. Add the sugar gradually to the egg yolks—a pastelike mixture will result. Slowly add the milk, stirring until well blended. Cook over medium-high heat, stirring constantly to prevent scorching. Continue stirring until the mixture has thickened. (You can tell because it will begin to boil as you stir, and there seems to be a lot more of it than when you started!) Remove from the heat, stir for 1 more minute, and then set aside and let cool.
3. Seal the vanilla wafers in a plastic freezer bag, then crumble them up using a kitchen mallet or rolling pin. Kids often like to take over this chore for you. Just make certain the cookies are *sealed* in the bag so crumbs don't fly everywhere. Set aside the sealed bag of crumbled cookies.
4. Drain the cherries through a sieve set over a 1-cup container. There shouldn't be enough juice to fill the container, so make up the difference by adding water. Add the gelatin to the cherry juice mixture and stir until the gelatin has dissolved; set aside.
5. Wearing rubber gloves to avoid staining your hands, cut the cherries in half; set aside. Chop the nuts into small chunks; set aside.
6. Beat the egg whites in the large mixing bowl until stiff peaks form. Add 1 tsp. of the vanilla to the cooked, cooled egg yolk mixture. Then stir in the cherries, the cherry juice mixture, the chopped nuts, and the crumbled vanilla wafers. Fold in

the beaten egg whites. Transfer the whole pudding to a large container or bowl. Cover and refrigerate at least 6 hours, preferably overnight.

7. Just before serving, beat the cream until stiff peaks form. Gently stir in the remaining 1 tsp. vanilla. Spoon the cold pudding into small bowls and top each serving with whipped cream. For fancy occasions, serve in stemmed glasses.

Christmas Plum Pudding

From England

PREPARE: *30 minutes* • STEAM: *3 hours* • SERVES: *12*

Throughout the ages, no holiday treat has been associated more closely with Christmas than English plum pudding. We love the tradition of plum pudding even though very few now serve it to their families and friends, and even fewer know that "plum pudding" has no plums in it at all! As I'll explain, the name comes from the old-fashioned way of preparing this delicacy.

If you would like to celebrate the Christmas season by serving its most venerable dessert, you can. We have switched some old-fashioned recipe components in favor of more readily available ingredients, but don't be offended by the change; even three hundred years ago, British plum pudding was already considerably different from the original, which even had a different name!

As far back as the fourteenth century, frumenty, a thick porridge of chopped beef or mutton mixed with fruit, wine, and spices, was a mainstay of Englishmen at Christmas. My friends and I certainly ate frumenty whenever it was offered to us, but the consistency was strange, and there was often a somewhat unpleasant aftertaste. Obviously, we weren't the only ones who noticed, for all through the 1500s cooks experimented with frumenty by adding new ingredients. Gradually it became the custom to mix in bread crumbs and eggs along with more fruit and less wine. Accordingly, over about two centuries the dish evolved from a thick soup to a thicker pudding, and eventually meat was removed from the recipe altogether, although there was still a significant amount of animal fat, or suet, included.

At that point, preparation changed radically. At Christmas, families would loosely wrap a mixture of suet, flour, dried fruits, nuts, and spices in cloth and boil the bundle until it became "plum," or expanded enough to tightly pack the cloth wrapper. That's where the name "plum pudding" comes from!

Plum pudding is always part of our North Pole holiday celebration. No wrapping of the ingredients in cloth is required, and Lars has done some tweaking to eliminate an in-

Lars Says: "At one time plum pudding was considered an extravagance and even sinful. When Puritans controlled the British government in the 1660s, they declared plum pudding to be 'unfit for God-fearing people' because of its rich ingredients. It actually was against the law to prepare or eat it, but after the Puritans were deposed, King George I reinstated the dish as part of the holiday season simply because he loved it so much. Good for him.

"For the plum pudding recipe I use at the North Pole, I substitute butter for suet. If you insist on entirely traditional ingredients, some specialty stores do sell 'vegetarian suet' made from palm oil and rice flour. Whether you use butter or suet, be very careful not to overcook the pudding; it dries out quite easily and is far less tasty.

"For a spectacular table presentation, douse the finished plum pudding with a little brandy and carefully ignite with a match. For something less inflammatory, forego the brandy and simply decorate the pudding with sprigs of holly, which you should caution your guests are not edible."

gredient that is hard to find—you won't pass a suet display in your local grocery store—without losing traditional consistency and taste. I heartily recommend this recipe to you!

¹/₂ (15-oz.) box of raisins
4 ozs. candied mixed fruit
4 ozs. lemon peel
brandy
1 cup (2 sticks) butter, at room temperature
¹/₂ cup packed brown sugar
4 eggs
2 cups all-purpose flour
¹/₂ tbsp. ground cinnamon
¹/₂ tbsp. ground allspice
1 tsp. baking powder
¹/₂ tsp. salt
1¹/₂ tbsp. brandy (optional, for presentation)
granulated sugar

1. Grease a large Pyrex bowl; set aside.
2. In a medium bowl, mix the raisins, candied fruit, and lemon peel. Pour in enough brandy to cover the mixture; set aside.
3. In another bowl, cream the butter and brown sugar. Add the eggs and stir until thoroughly mixed and smooth; set aside.
4. Sift the flour, cinnamon, allspice, baking powder, and salt. Add the flour mixture and the fruit mixture alternately to the creamed butter mixture, stirring in a little

of each until all the ingredients are combined. Pour the pudding mixture into the prepared bowl. Cover the top tightly with a double layer of waxed paper and a layer of foil. Tie snugly with string around the rim to seal.

5. Place the bowl in a pot that is large enough and wide enough to easily accommodate it. Add enough boiling water to reach a level about 3 inches from the top of the sealed bowl. Return to boiling over high heat. Reduce the heat to medium, cover the pot, and steam the pudding for 3 hours, adding hot water as necessary to maintain the water level in the pot.

6. Transfer the plum pudding from the Pyrex bowl to a serving dish. If you wish, drizzle the pudding with the 1½ tbsp. brandy. Sprinkle with granulated sugar. Light the brandy; the sugar will caramelize and add a delightful crunch to the overall consistency of the dessert.

Holiday Plum Pie Cookies

From the North Pole

PREPARE: *20 minutes* • BAKE: *10 minutes*
SERVES: *4 to 6 (3 cookies per person)*

If you're determined to have plums as part of a Christmas season dessert, you can't go wrong with this tasty recipe, which harks back to the Middle Ages. Back then, people didn't have any modern conveniences, including refrigerators to keep food fresh and fancy pots in which to cook it. Rather, they created tasty, simple dishes that required very little preparation time and called for the most common of ingredients: fruit, flour, sugar, salt, and, common for those times, suet.

Lars once again has put his own unique spin on this tradition. The result is plum pie cookies, which are absolutely delectable and so easy to prepare. There's something about the sensation of biting into one, when your teeth break through flaky, sweet crust to encounter the slight tartness of diced plum, that will definitely make your day seem merry and bright.

Lars Says: *"I've again substituted butter for suet. While this is a simple recipe, be careful not to overwork the dough. If you do, the dough won't mold properly around the diced plums.*

"I've found this to be the perfect recipe for keeping children happily occupied during the last frantic hours before Christmas Eve. And I can promise you that Santa will be thrilled if there are plum pie cookies waiting for him when it's finally time to place presents under your family's Christmas tree!"

2 fresh plums
6 tbsp. granulated sugar
2 tbsp. brown sugar
$\frac{1}{2}$ tbsp. ground cinnamon
$1\frac{1}{2}$ tbsp. honey
$1\frac{3}{4}$ cups all-purpose flour
1 tsp. salt
$\frac{1}{2}$ cup (1 stick) butter, room temperature,
    cut into small pieces
1 egg yolk
4 tbsp. water
1 tbsp. fresh lemon juice

1. Preheat your oven to 425°F. Grease a large cookie sheet; set aside.
2. Prepare the filling: Halve the plums and remove the pits. Chop into small pieces. Transfer the plums to a medium bowl. Add 2 tbsp. of the granulated sugar, all the brown sugar, cinnamon, and honey and toss until well mixed; set aside.
3. Prepare the dough: Using a fork, mix the flour, salt, and butter in a large bowl, until the mixture resembles coarse crumbs. In a separate bowl, mix the egg yolk, 3 tbsp. of the water, and the lemon juice. Stirring with a fork, slowly add the egg mixture to the flour mixture; stir until the mixture comes together, forming a dough.
4. On a lightly floured surface, roll out the dough as thinly as possible without tearing it. Using a 1 1/2-inch circular cookie cutter, cut out 2 rounds of the dough. Place a small spoonful of plum filling in the center of one round. Wet the edges of the round with water, and cover with the second round. Seal by pressing the edges together with a fork, creating a pleasant crimped pattern. When the edges are completely sealed, use a sharp knife to cut two small steam holes on top. Repeat until you have used all the dough and filling. There should be 12 to 18 cookies.
5. Place the cookies on the prepared cookie sheet and bake for about 7 minutes or until the tops of the cookies just begin to brown. Remove the cookie sheet from the oven and transfer it to a wire rack or trivet, leaving the oven on.
6. In a small bowl, mix the remaining 2 tbsp. granulated sugar with the remaining 1 tbsp. water. Drizzle this mixture over the cookies, then return the cookie sheet to the oven and bake for about 3 more minutes, or until the tops of the cookies are completely browned. Transfer the cookie sheet to a wire rack and let cookies cool on the sheet for 5 minutes before serving.

Black Christmas Fruitcake

From Trinidad and Tobago

PREPARE: *at least overnight* • BAKE: *2 ½ hours* • SERVES: *12 (3 loaves)*

It's not true that everyone hates Christmas fruitcake. Most people simply haven't had the opportunity to taste the version that's a holiday tradition in the twin-island nation of Trinidad and Tobago, where the weather is sunny and warm when Christmas arrives. Contrary to what you might expect, tropical weather does not inhibit holiday spirits. *Parang* carolers stroll from house to house, banging on instruments ranging from guitars to pots and pans and singing festive songs reflecting the calypso music of the region. Everyone is caught up in the festive spirit; there's no such thing as *parang* revelers arriving too late to be invited in for snacks and holiday fellowship.

On Christmas Day itself, families in Trinidad and Tobago gather for a celebratory dinner whose main course might be turkey, ham, or pork, but whose dessert is inevitably everyone's favorite: Black Christmas Fruitcake. This dish is admittedly rather complicated to prepare, but no one considers the work to be drudgery. Rather, it's part of the overall enjoyment of the holiday, and the result is frankly astounding: a dark, rich fruitcake full of overlapping bold and subtle flavors and nothing like the bland, dry product that too many of us associate with fruitcakes in general.

Because of its lengthy preparation, we never expect Lars and his kitchen staff to serve more than one Black Christmas Fruitcake per holiday season at the North Pole, but what a joyous day it is when Lars presents us with these loaves. I think this cake would be a special hit at holiday parties. After you try this one, you'll never make fun of fruitcake again.

Lars Says: "*While it's acceptable to prepare this recipe with a fruit mixture soaked overnight in rum and brandy, tradition suggests you should store it in your pantry (but not your refrigerator!) for at least a week and preferably for a month. It really takes time for all the flavors to blend.*

"*Black Christmas Fruitcake also requires a special spice mix that needs to be prepared in advance. I've broken out that portion of the recipe to make it easier to follow. The 'mixed peel' for the fruit mixture should be readily available in most grocery stores. You can certainly pick up cherry brandy and Trinidad rum at most liquor stores.*

"*This one's a real challenge, even for experienced chefs. But I suspect anyone who loves Christmas will be up to it!*"

THE MIXED SPICES:

6 tsp. ground coriander

5 tsp. ground cinnamon

4 tsp. ground allspice

3 tsp. ground nutmeg

2 tsp. ground ginger

1 tsp. ground cloves

THE FRUIT MIXTURE:

$^1/_2$ lb. prunes

$^1/_2$ lb. raisins

$^1/_2$ lb. currants

2 ozs. mixed peel

$^1/_4$ lb. cherries

$^1/_2$ lb. almonds, chopped

$^1/_2$ (375-ml) bottle cherry brandy

$^1/_8$ (375-ml) bottle Trinidad rum

1 tbsp. angostura bitters

THE BROWNING SAUCE:

$1^1/_2$ cups packed brown sugar

$^1/_4$ cup hot water

THE FRUITCAKE BATTER:

1 cup (2 sticks) butter, room temperature

$1^1/_8$ cups sugar

4 large eggs

$^1/_2$ tsp. lemon extract

1 tsp. freshly grated lime rind

1 tsp. almond extract
1 tsp. vanilla extract
1 tsp. mixed spices (see recipe above)
2 cups all-purpose flour
2 tsp. baking powder
¼ tsp. ground nutmeg

1. Combine all the mixed spice ingredients in a medium bowl and stir with a fork until well blended. Transfer to an airtight container and store in a cool, dry place until needed.

2. Chop up all the fruit. Combine the chopped fruit and the almonds in a plastic, resealable bag. Add the brandy, rum, and bitters. Seal the bag and let the mixture soak in the refrigerator at least overnight or as long as one month.

3. On the day you intend to serve the fruitcake, begin by making the sauce: Heat the brown sugar in a small saucepan over low heat until the sugar burns. Remove the pan from the heat and slowly add the hot water; set the pan aside.

4. Preheat your oven to 250°F. Grease three 9½ by 5½–inch loaf pans. Line each pan with a double sheet of parchment paper; set aside.

5. Prepare the batter: In a large mixing bowl, cream the butter and sugar. One at a time, add the eggs, stirring until blended after adding each egg. One by one, add the lemon extract, lime rind, almond extract, and vanilla, stirring constantly to ensure an even mix; set aside.

6. Sift the flour, baking powder, mixed spices, and nutmeg into a medium bowl. Gradually add this mixture to the creamed butter and sugar, stirring

until blended. Stir in the marinated fruit, and then the browning sauce; mix *thoroughly*.

7. Divide the batter among the three prepared loaf pans. Bake for about 2½ hours. Test with a knife. If it pulls out clean, the fruitcake is done.

8. Remove the loaves from the oven and transfer to wire racks. Let stand for 10 minutes. Then transfer the fruitcakes to serving platters. If you like, drizzle the cakes with more cherry brandy before serving. This fruitcake is anything but boring and bland!

Fruitcake Cookies

From the North Pole

PREPARE: *15 minutes plus 20 minutes for cooling*
BAKE: *15 to 20 minutes* • SERVES: *12 (4 cookies per person)*

Did you know that fruitcake dates back to early Egyptian times? Well before even Santa Claus was born, Egyptians are believed to have baked fruit and spices into bread and then placed the loaves in tombs to help deceased loved ones make the transition to the afterlife. No wonder fruitcake has had such an unfortunate reputation for so long!

Later, Roman soldiers carried fruitcake in their packs on long marches. It wasn't until the 1700s that it became associated with holidays rather than less festive events like funerals and battles. Fruitcake finally became part of the Christmas tradition in the 1700s, when rich families would distribute slices to carolers and less fortunate families. This practice evolved into sending fruitcake as a gift, since it was well preserved and could withstand shipping.

Lars has developed a fabulous recipe for Fruitcake Cookies that would make even Egyptians and Roman legionnaires beg for second helpings. Cookies didn't come along until later, probably around the seventh century in Persia. Here, Lars combines cookie and fruitcake ingredients in a single tasty confection that every modern holiday reveler will love.

Lars Says: *"People unfairly associate the term* fruitcake *with heavy food that rests uncomfortably like lead in your stomach. That's why I enjoy preparing these delicious, light cookies, which prove that fruitcake can be enjoyed as a delectable snack that won't spoil appetites or ruin digestion.*

"While I suggest you use citron in this recipe, please feel free to substitute candied lemon or orange. And don't forget to let these cookies cool a bit before you serve them; they taste much better that way."

2 tsp. baking soda

1 1/2 tbsp. whole milk

1 1/2 cups all-purpose flour

1/2 tsp. ground allspice

1/2 tsp. ground cloves

1/2 tsp. ground cinnamon

1/2 tsp. ground nutmeg

1/2 lb. candied cherries

1/2 lb. candied pineapple

1/2 lb. candied citron (or candied lemon or orange)

1/4 cup (1/2 stick) butter, room temperature

1/2 cup packed brown sugar

2 eggs, well beaten

⅓ cup grape jelly
1 lb. pecans, chopped
1 lb. raisins

1. Preheat your oven to 300°F. Lightly grease a cookie sheet; set aside.
2. In a small bowl, with a fork, mix the baking soda and the milk until the baking soda has dissolved; set aside.
3. In a medium bowl, with a wire whisk, stir the flour, allspice, cloves, cinnamon, and nutmeg until blended; set aside.
4. Chop the candied cherries, pineapple, and citron into small pieces; set aside.
5. In a large mixing bowl, cream the butter and brown sugar. Stir in the eggs and grape jelly until well mixed. Add the flour mixture, the chopped candied fruit, the pecans, and the raisins. Add the baking soda mixture last. Stir until you have a batter.
6. Drop the batter by teaspoonfuls on the prepared cookie sheet. Because they will not expand much as they bake, you can place the cookies fairly close together. Bake for 15 to 20 minutes, or until lightly browned. If you take out the cookies before they've browned, they'll taste doughy. If you let them bake until they are dark brown on top, they'll be too hard. A light brown fruitcake cookie will have a delicate crunch to it. Transfer the cookies to a wire rack and let cool 20 minutes before serving.

Kahk (Sweet Cookies)

From Egypt

PREPARE: *20 minutes plus 65 minutes total resting time*
BAKE: *15 minutes* • SERVES: *6 (3 per person)*

They do love Christmas—and cookies—in Egypt! Because of calendar differences, Egyptians celebrate Christmas on our January 7, and tasty *kahk* cookies are usually part of the festivities. Since most Egyptian Christians observe a limited fast from November 25 through January 6, consuming vegetables but no meat or dairy products, they really enjoy their favorite holiday dessert afterward!

Kahk cross other theological boundaries: They are also favored by Muslims, who use them to break their own holiday-related fasts. Egyptian Christians like to decorate theirs with crosses. At the North Pole, Lars sometimes uses icing to draw more secular motifs like reindeer or Christmas trees.

Lars Says: *"The preparation isn't complicated, but the steps must be followed precisely, especially the instruction to let the uncooked* kahk *rest for about 5 minutes before placing in the oven.*

"Because Santa is so very fond of icing, it's true I sometimes add it to kahk. *But they taste best when simply sprinkled with powdered sugar."*

2 cups (4 sticks) unsalted butter
4 ½ cups all-purpose flour
2 tbsp. baking powder
1 tsp. ground cinnamon
1 tsp. ground cloves
1 tsp. ground ginger
1 tsp. fast-rising instant yeast
1 cup whole milk
1 tsp. granulated sugar
powdered sugar

THE FILLING:

walnuts (chopped or whole)
honey
date spread

1. In a small saucepan, heat the butter to almost boiling; remove from the heat.
2. In a medium bowl, combine the flour, baking powder, cinnamon, cloves, and ginger. Slowly add the hot butter, stirring until thoroughly blended.
3. In a small bowl, mix the instant yeast, milk, and granulated sugar. Add the yeast mixture to the butter mixture, stirring gently until a dough is formed. The dough should be cool to the touch. Knead gently for 5 to 10 minutes, then cover and allow to rest for 1 hour.
4. Preheat your oven to 345°F.
5. Shape the *kahk* dough into 1-inch balls, and then flatten them with your hand.

Insert a small amount of the filling of your choice—walnuts, honey, or date spread—and then roll the *kahk* around the filling back into a ball. Place the balls on a cookie sheet lined with parchment paper and allow to rest for 5 minutes. Don't skip this step.

6. Bake for about 15 minutes or until golden brown. Cool completely on a wire rack. Just before serving, dust with powdered sugar.

Pavlova (Holiday Meringue)

From New Zealand

PREPARE: *25 minutes plus overnight for cooling*
BAKE: *2 hours* • SERVES: *8*

We always try to avoid controversy at the North Pole, but I must introduce this recipe with an admission: Both New Zealand and Australia claim to be the country of origin for this dessert, which is a popular Christmas treat in each place. Santa Claus never takes sides, so please don't take my attribution of Pavlova to New Zealand as favoritism. It's just that one Christmas long ago it was in New Zealand that I first tasted this sweet dish, and I have loved it ever since. I mean no disrespect to my Australian friends.

Christmas in New Zealand is a very special occasion. In many towns, I don't arrive by sleigh but by fire engine, with sirens sounding as the signal for children to run up and receive gifts of candy. December there is the middle of summer, so holiday fare is often lighter than that in other parts of the world. There are festive Christmas barbecues and afterward desserts that often feature delicious kiwifruit. Meringuelike Pavlova garnished with kiwi or strawberries is everyone's favorite, and once you try it you'll never want to spend a Pavlova-less Christmas again.

Lara Says: *"Pavlova isn't difficult to prepare, but you must remember to beat the egg whites until they are stiff; anything less, and the dessert won't be crunchy on the outside and creamy on the inside.*

"Don't forget to let the Pavlova sit overnight. This is a crucial step and one that absolutely cannot be ignored. It's a problem for me at the North Pole because Santa often can't wait that long and tries to raid the kitchen before the Pavlova is ready—that's how much he loves it!"

3 egg whites
pinch of salt
3/4 cup powdered sugar
1/4 cup granulated sugar
1 tbsp. cornstarch
1 tsp. fresh lemon juice
1 1/3 cups heavy cream, whipped
sliced fresh kiwi or strawberries for garnish, as much as you please
   (Santa is pleased by much!)

1. Preheat your oven to 300°F. Line a cookie sheet with parchment; set aside.
2. In a medium bowl, beat the egg whites until foamy. Add the salt and beat until soft peaks form. Continue beating while you gradually add the powdered sugar. You're done beating when stiff peaks stand up rather than fold over when the beaters are lifted.

3. In a small separate bowl, with a fork, stir the granulated sugar and cornstarch. Gently fold this mixture into the meringue, then add the lemon juice.

4. On the prepared cookie sheet, using a spoon-shaped spatula, spread the meringue in a rough circle. Place the tray in the oven and *immediately* reduce the heat to 180°F. Bake for 2 hours. Turn off the heat and leave the meringue in the oven overnight for 8 to 12 hours.

5. When ready to serve, top the Pavlova with whipped cream and garnish with the kiwi or strawberries or both. The outside of the Pavlova will have formed a sugary, crunchy shell, and the inside should be smooth and creamy. Just like Santa, all your guests will want seconds and probably thirds.

Kulkuls (Coconut Cookies)

From India

PREPARE: *15 minutes plus 15 minutes for cooling* • FRY: *10 minutes*

SERVES: *7 to 8 (4 per person)*

India is one of my favorite countries for Christmas Eve gift-giving. There are enough Christians there who celebrate the holiday to create wonderful seasonal traditions. It's thrilling to visit cities like Bombay and Delhi, where candlelight parades fill the streets, and just as exciting to make my way to smaller villages, where everyone gathers to sing carols. But I confess that what I enjoy most are the *kulkul*s left out by children who want to offer me a delicious snack for my long night's labors.

*Kulkul*s are simple coconut-flavored cookies that melt in your mouth. They're easy to prepare, and many mothers in Indian families ask their children to help make them. Your family will enjoy both the experience and the cookies that result.

2 cups all-purpose flour
pinch of salt
½ tbsp. butter, room temperature
1 egg, lightly beaten
1½ tbsp. powdered sugar plus a little more for dusting
½ cup coconut milk
2 cups oil for frying (Lars prefers olive oil, but any vegetable oil
*   will do.)*

1. Line a cookie sheet with a double layer of paper towels; set aside.
2. Sift the flour and salt into a large bowl. Add the butter, mixing gently. Stir in the egg. Then add the powdered sugar and coconut milk and stir until a soft, pliable dough is formed.
3. Using your hands, form the dough into 1-inch balls. Grease the tines of a fork and flatten out the dough balls to form rectangles measuring roughly 2 inches by 1 inch.

Then roll up the flattened dough, from one long side to the other, into wide, tight curls.

4. Heat the oil in a heavy deep pan over medium heat. Fry the *kulkul*s, turning them constantly, for about 10 minutes, until they are golden brown all over. Using a slotted spoon, transfer the *kulkul*s as they are done to the prepared cookie sheet; set aside to drain for 15 minutes before serving. They're tasty either warm or cold.

Cassata Siciliana
(Sicilian Spongε Cakε)

From Italy

PREPARE: *45 minutes* • BAKE: *30 minutes for the sponge cake*

SERVES: *8*

For centuries, children in Italy have awaited January 6 and the annual visit of La Befana, a wizened old woman who missed her original chance to visit Baby Jesus with the Wise Men and who has been bringing gifts to good boys and girls since. But modern times have yielded a newer tradition: a Christmas Eve visit from Babbo Natale, as I'm known to Italians.

I love sharing the gift-giving excitement with Befana! In some regions of Italy, the early holiday season is ushered in by *zampognari* (bagpipers), and everyone enjoys anticipating Natale on December 25. We've discussed elsewhere the fabulous *presepi*, or manger scenes, that many Italian families place in their homes. What a Christmas-loving nation!

Naturally, Italian holiday festivities include wonderful foods, and none more fabulous than *Cassata Siciliana*, the most delectable sponge cake I have ever tasted, and at my age, I believe I may have tasted every possible variation! The frosting, in particular, is scrumptious almost beyond description.

Lara Says: "*This recipe seems more difficult than it actually is. At the North Pole, I like to serve* Cassata Siciliana *on January 6 after everyone has returned from helping La Befana make her Epiphany gift-giving rounds. That makes it a special treat.*

"*You can, of course, buy a sponge cake and make your own frosting. That would save you some time and trouble, but I promise that if you follow the complete recipe, your homemade cake will taste far superior to anything from a bakery!*

"*The sponge cake recipe makes two cakes. Use one now and freeze the other for a future holiday treat.*"

THE SPONGE CAKE (for two cakes; use only one for *Cassata Siciliana*):

1 cup (2 sticks) butter, room temperature

1 cup sugar

4 eggs

2 cups all-purpose flour

2 tsp. baking powder

THE FROSTING:

3 cups ricotta cheese

¹/₂ cup sugar

4 tbsp. medium-dry sherry

pinch of ground cinnamon (less than a tsp.)

¹/₂ cup mixed peel, finely chopped

4 ozs. semisweet chocolate
1 1/2 tbsp. cold water
6 glacé or maraschino cherries

1. Preheat your oven to 375°F. Grease two 8-inch round baking pans; set aside.
2. In a large bowl, cream butter. Slowly add sugar, beating until light and fluffy. Add eggs one at a time; stir until well mixed. Sift flour and baking powder; fold in.
3. Pour the batter into the prepared pans. Bake for 25 to 30 minutes, until each cake pulls away from the sides of the pan and a cake tester inserted into the middle of each cake comes out clean. Transfer the pans to a wire rack and let the cakes cool *in* the pans for 10 minutes. Then remove them from the pans and cool completely on a wire rack. You'll need only 1 cake for this dessert.
4. While the cakes are cooling, stir the ricotta cheese, 1/4 cup of the sugar, and 2 tbsp. of the sherry in a medium bowl until the mixture is smooth and well blended. Stir in the cinnamon and mixed peel.
5. Cut 2 ozs. of the chocolate into tiny pieces. Add to the ricotta mixture. Taste for sweetness; add sugar if you wish.
6. Cut one cooled sponge cake in half *horizontally*. Mix the remaining 2 tbsp. sherry with the cold water and sprinkle over the cut side of each half. The cake should be moist but not too wet. Place one half, cut side up, on a cake plate and spread evenly with half of the cheese mixture. Then cover with the other half of the cake, cut side down. Cover the top and sides of the cake with the remaining cheese mixture.
7. Using a sharp knife, shave the remaining 2 ozs. chocolate into thin curls. Garnish the top of the cake with the curls and the cherries. Slice and serve.

Buñuelos
(Cinnamon-Sugar Sticks)

From Mexico

PREPARE: *15 minutes plus 1 hour for resting of the dough*
COOK: *15 minutes* • SERVES: *8 (3 per person)*

Some of the simplest international holiday dishes are also the tastiest. *Buñuelos,* the popular Mexican Christmas treat, are wonderful examples.

As we discussed earlier, holiday celebrations in Mexico are quite elaborate, with Las Posadas processions nine nights in a row, Misa de Gallo masses, and extended Christmas meals that can include a dozen courses and last almost as many hours. In contrast, preparing a batch of *buñuelos* is as easy as wishing someone *"Feliz Navidad."* These cookielike treats will please the orneriest Christmas Scrooge, and they're the perfect solution to the problem of what to bring to last-minute holiday parties or family gatherings.

I do fancy myself quite the expert on all things cookie-related, and I promise you that during my Christmas Eve rounds, a plate of *buñuelos* certainly qualifies as one of Santa's favorite seasonal treats!

1½ cups sifted all-purpose flour
½ tbsp. sugar
½ tsp. baking powder
¼ tsp. salt
1 egg, well beaten
2 tbsp. butter, melted
¼ cup milk
shortening
oil for frying
cinnamon-sugar

1. Line a large cookie sheet with a double layer of paper towels; set aside.
2. Sift the flour, sugar, baking powder, and salt into a medium bowl. Add the beaten egg and melted butter, and enough of the milk to form a soft (but not sticky) dough. Transfer the dough to a floured board and knead until the dough

is smooth and a little glossy. Brush the dough with shortening and allow to rest for 1 hour.

3. To begin the cooking process, pinch off walnut-size pieces of dough. Roll each piece on a floured board to the thinness of paper. Allow the rolled-out *buñuelos* to stand while you heat the oil in a deep heavy pan. When the oil is very hot (375°F on a deep-fat thermometer), carefully drop in the *buñuelos*. They should float on the surface of the oil rather than sink. Fry the *buñuelos*, turning once, until they are golden brown on both sides. Using a slotted spoon, transfer the *buñuelos* as they are done to the prepared cookie sheet to drain.

4. Sprinkle both sides with cinnamon-sugar. Serve warm or cold.

Holiday *Beigli*
(Poppy Seed or Walnut Pastries)

From Hungary

PREPARE: *30 minutes plus 2 to 3 hours for rising of the dough*
BAKE: *45 minutes* • SERVES: *6*

In Hungary, children eagerly await a December 6 visit from Mikulás Bácsi, or Uncle Nicholas, and I'm so happy to oblige. Some of the boys and girls leave out boots for me to fill with candy and other treats. Others hope I'll leave them gifts wrapped in red paper—the traditional color of holiday wrapping paper in Hungary. Afterward, many of the children place my gifts on their windowsills, so passersby will see proof that the youngsters within have been good all year. Parents tell children who've been naughty that I might leave them a bundle of twigs or a switch instead, but I have never had to actually do this. Rather than risk my displeasure, these boys and girls immediately change their ways for the better.

After my early-December visit, Hungarian holiday observances continue. Many towns stage a Betlehemezés, or "Bethlehem Play," that reenacts the birth of Jesus. On Christmas Eve, there is "the visiting of shepherds." From sunset until midnight, groups carrying shepherds' crooks wander the streets, knocking on friends' doors, and singing Christmas carols. Usually, they are invited in for drinks and snacks.

On Christmas Eve, children find more gifts, these brought to them by Jézuska, or Baby

Jesus, and his angels. Early in the afternoon on Christmas Day, families gather for dinner. Fish is the most popular main course, and only *beigli* will do for dessert. These filled cookies delight Hungarians, and I believe your family will agree—*if* you are all fond of poppy seeds! To be on the safe side, Lars also offers a walnut *beigli* variation.

𝕃ars 𝕊ays: "This recipe is rather complicated, so be prepared to spend a little extra time when you first attempt it. The walnut version is also used in Hungary, though poppy seed beigli *are more traditional.*

"Make certain the beigli *are completely baked before removing them from the oven. Don't forget to use a fork to poke air holes in the tops; improperly prepared* beigli *can be soggy. The steam inside needs to escape."*

THE PASTRY:

1 pkg. dry yeast
1 tsp. granulated sugar
¼ cup lukewarm whole milk
4 cups all-purpose flour
⅓ cup powdered sugar
¼ tsp. salt
¾ cup (1½ sticks) butter, room temperature
3 eggs, separated
¼ to ½ cup whole milk

THE POPPY SEED FILLING:

2 cups poppy seeds
³/₄ cup whole milk
1 cup granulated sugar
2 tbsp. apricot jam
1 tsp. honey
grated rind of ¹/₂ lemon

THE WALNUT FILLING:

3 cups walnuts
1 cup granulated sugar
¹/₂ cup water
grated rind of ¹/₂ lemon

1. Prepare the dough: In a medium bowl, combine the yeast, granulated sugar, and lukewarm milk; stir until the yeast has dissolved. Set aside.

2. Combine the flour, powdered sugar, and salt in a large bowl and whisk until blended. Mix in the softened butter. Scoop out a well in the center of the mixture. Pour the yeast mixture and 3 egg yolks into the well and mix gently, gradually adding between ¹/₄ and ¹/₂ cup of milk until the dough forms a ball. Cover the dough with a cloth; place in a warm, draft-free spot and let rise until the dough has about doubled in size. This will take 2 to 3 hours.

3. Meanwhile, prepare the fillings: Grind the poppy seeds and/or walnuts as finely as possible. You can chop rather than grind them, but make sure the bits are as small as you can make them. This is a dessert to be *chewed* rather than *crunched*.

4. Mix all the ingredients for either one of the two fillings or for both in separate medium saucepans. Simmer, stirring frequently, over low heat for about 15 minutes. Remove from the heat and set aside to cool.

5. Preheat your oven to 350°F.

6. Divide the dough in half. Roll out each half on a floured surface into an approximately 12 by 18–inch rectangle. Spread the fillings evenly on the dough rectangles, leaving about a 1-inch margin on the edges. Turn up the sides to prevent leakage and, beginning from one long side, roll up the *beigli* jelly-roll fashion. You should end up with two 12-inch-long rolls.

7. Brush the tops of the rolls with beaten egg whites, then use a fork to poke a few air holes in the tops. Bake for 40 to 45 minutes, or until the *beigli* are golden brown. Transfer to a wire rack and let cool for 15 minutes. Cut crosswise into sections and serve.

Yuletide *Aloco* (Plantain Chips)

From Ivory Coast

PREPARE: *10 minutes* • COOK: *10 minutes* • SERVES: 6

About twenty-five percent of the citizens of Ivory Coast are Christians who celebrate Christmas. Most live in a few big cities where French is the most common spoken language. Accordingly, many French holiday customs are observed, including displays of elaborate nativity scenes in homes, much-anticipated Christmas Eve visits from Père Noël (that's me!), and on Christmas Eve after Midnight Mass a festive family meal known as *réveillon*.

Another Christmas custom observed in Ivory Coast is the offering of special holiday snacks to family, friends, and unexpected visitors. Here, the fare is somewhat more unique to the country itself. One of my favorites, and something often left out for me on Christmas Eve by native boys and girls, is *aloco*, a very simple chip made from specially prepared slices of plantain.

When I mentioned *aloco* to Lars, he immediately fixed a batch for my North Pole friends, and they loved them, too. One of the advantages of *aloco* is that it can be prepared in a matter of minutes and is usually enjoyed by holiday revelers of all ages. This Christmas season, give *aloco* a try!

4 firm, ripe plantains (not bananas!)
1 cup vegetable oil
2 tbsp. sugar

1. Line a cookie sheet with a double layer of paper towels; set aside.
2. Peel the plantains and cut them crosswise into $^1/_4$-inch-thick slices.
3. Heat the vegetable oil in a large, heavy skillet over medium-high heat until hot (375°F on a deep-fat thermometer). Add a few plantain slices at a time and fry them for 3 minutes on each side. The outer skin will turn golden brown, but the inside will stay soft. Using a slotted spoon, transfer them as they are done to the prepared cookie sheet and set aside to drain.
4. When the *aloco* are *thoroughly* drained, sprinkle them with the sugar and keep them warm until ready to serve. Now, *there's* an easy recipe!

White House Christmas "Moose"

From the U.S.A.

PREPARE: *20 minutes plus 1 hour for cooling* • COOK: *20 minutes*
SERVES: *6 to 8, depending on size of helpings*

When my dear old friend Theodore Roosevelt lived in the White House as president, he had to preside over countless holiday dinners and receptions. Theodore was not then and still is not now someone comfortable with social or prandial flourishes. He's plainspoken and likes his food simple, too.

This caused problems. When White House cooks presented him with delicacies in particularly tiny portions, Theodore would rebel. He liked Christmas desserts that tasted good and were filling enough to satisfy his hearty appetite. Theodore took over the White House kitchen himself and eventually concocted what he called White House Christmas Moose. He meant "mousse," of course, but "moose" was always one of his favorite words as well as a favorite animal.

The ingredients are easy to track down, and the raspberry liqueur is optional. It certainly adds to the festive flavor and texture, but we leave that to you. When you and your friends enjoy this dish, please remember that Theodore Roosevelt wishes you a very Merry Christmas!

½ lb. good-quality dark cooking chocolate, broken into chunks
1 cup milk
2 tbsp. butter
1 tsp. vanilla extract
1 tsp. corn syrup
⅔ cup raspberry liqueur (Chambord is good.)
2 cups granulated sugar (approximately)
½ cup packed brown sugar
½ lb. fresh raspberries, crushed and chopped
whipped cream
several whole raspberries, at least 1 for each serving

1. Using a double boiler, heat the chocolate with the milk over barely simmering water until completely melted and smooth. While stirring constantly, add the butter, vanilla, corn syrup, raspberry liqueur, and granulated and brown sugars. If the mixture becomes too thick for easy stirring, add a little more milk. Cook for at least 15 minutes.

2. Add the crushed raspberries and taste. If you find the mixture to be too bitter, add extra sugar. Cook for 5 more minutes.

3. Using a small ladle, divide the mixture equally among 6 to 8 small dessert bowls (or, if Theodore Roosevelt happens to be your guest, 2 or 3 large ones). Let stand for at least 1 hour. Before serving, top each portion with whipped cream and a whole raspberry.

Candy Cane *Crème Brûlée*

From the North Pole

PREPARE: *20 minutes plus about 5 hours chilling*
(It's best to prepare this dessert the day before you intend to serve it.)
COOK: *25 to 30 minutes* • SERVES: *6*

Crème brûlée first became popular as a holiday treat sometime in the late 1600s or early 1700s. Cooking historians disagree on whether this delicious delight originated in France, England, or Spain. I frankly don't think it matters; can there be anyone anywhere who doesn't enjoy *crème brûlée*?

The name by which it is best known may indicate where the dish was invented: *crème brûlée* is French for "burned cream." (Spaniards prefer to call it *crema catalana*.) This particular recipe might be said to have come to us via France by way of the North Pole. There is something especially festive about the taste of peppermint, and Lars has demonstrated his usual deft holiday touch by inventing this particular recipe. From the time he first served it to me and my friends, it has been a North Pole favorite.

We realize that preparing *crème brûlée* takes some time and a delicate touch, so we don't expect Lars to serve it more than once every Christmas season. We suggest you reserve this stunning treat for a very special holiday dinner.

Lara Says: "*Crème brûlée is scrumptious. The wonderful crunch you feel when you break through the hardened sugar shell on top always reminds me of walking over a crust of fresh snow on Christmas morning at the North Pole.*

"*There are two important things to remember when cooking this or any other variation of* crème brûlée. *First, do not overfill the dish with custard. A very shallow depth, of no more than ¾ inch and preferably about ½ inch, is ideal. This means shallow, wide, flameproof dishes (ramekins) work best. Second, always cook* crème brûlée *s-l-o-w-l-y.*

"*Caramelize the sugar on top with a small blowtorch, which you can buy at most kitchen stores.*"

3 cups heavy or whipping cream
6 large egg yolks
⅓ cup crushed candy canes
½ tsp. peppermint extract
3 tbsp. sugar
6 mini candy canes for garnish (optional)

SPECIAL EQUIPMENT:

6 flameproof ramekins
small blowtorch (available in most kitchen stores)

1. Place a rack in the middle of your oven and preheat to 325°F.
2. In a kettle, bring 3 cups of water to a boil over high heat.
3. Meanwhile, heat the cream in a saucepan over medium heat, stirring occasionally, until the cream is hot but not boiling. Remove from the heat and set aside.
4. In a medium bowl, whisk the egg yolks and crushed candy canes until well mixed. Then, whisking continuously, *slowly* add the hot cream until blended. Stir in the peppermint extract.
5. Place 6 ramekins in a roasting pan. Spoon the custard mixture into the ramekins, being careful to wipe off any spilled drops with a damp cloth.
6. Remove the kettle from the heat and fill the roasting pan with enough boiling water to reach halfway up the ramekins. Then carefully place the roasting pan on the oven rack and bake for no longer than 25 to 30 minutes, until the custard has set.
7. Remove the ramekins from the roasting pan and place them on a wire rack. When they have cooled to room temperature, cover them with plastic wrap or foil and refrigerate for at least 5 hours.
8. About 10 minutes before serving, sprinkle each custard evenly with the sugar and use a kitchen blowtorch to caramelize the sugar. If you haven't done this before, it's easier than it sounds. Just move the flame back and forth just above the sugar. Let stand for about 5 minutes or until the caramelized sugar hardens. If you like, garnish with small whole or crushed candy canes. Then serve!

Holiday Black Walnut Cake

From Germany

PREPARE: *45 minutes plus* five days *afterward!* • BAKE: *25 minutes*
SERVES: *12*

If you think it seems to take forever for Christmas Day to arrive, wait until you're anticipating a delicious slice of homemade Holiday Black Walnut Cake! This traditional German sweet is one of the most delectable holiday desserts in history, but patience is one of the crucial ingredients. Some recipes require you to wait a few hours while dough is rising. This cake must be left undisturbed for five whole days after it is baked!

My North Pole friends and I have been enjoying this dessert for centuries. Almost any cake is pleasant to eat, and various walnut cakes have been common in Europe since Persians brought walnuts to Italy two thousand or so years ago. The Romans first singled out walnuts as special; at one point they believed their gods ate walnuts while lesser mortals had to settle for acorns. But the Germanic people soon became fond of walnuts, too. Any time of year, German bakeries offer dozens of walnut-flavored delicacies. On December 6, German children hope that Saint Nicholas will leave walnuts in their stockings along with candy and fruit. And as Christmas Day approaches, many families hope to celebrate with slices of Holiday Black Walnut Cake.

I cannot properly describe the wonders of this cake. When it is baked properly, and left in an airtight container for the requisite five days, its varied flavors first explode in your mouth and then linger pleasantly on your taste buds. It is a dessert experience that you and your family simply must indulge in once every holiday season.

❄

THE CAKE:

5 eggs, separated

3 cups all-purpose flour

3 tsp. baking powder

1/4 tsp. salt

2 cups granulated sugar

1 cup shortening

1 cup whole milk

3/4 cup chopped black walnuts

2 tsp. vanilla extract

THE ICING:

9 tbsp. butter

6 tbsp. heavy or whipping cream

6 cups powdered sugar

3 tsp. vanilla extract

1. Preheat your oven to 350°F. Cut circles of waxed paper to fit the bottom of four 8-inch round cake pans. Place the paper in the pans, lightly grease the paper and the sides of the pans, and dust with flour; set aside.
2. In a large bowl, beat the egg whites until stiff peaks form; set aside.
3. Sift the flour, baking powder, and salt into a large bowl.
4. In a medium bowl, cream the granulated sugar and shortening. Add the sugar mixture to the sifted flour mixture and beat until smooth. Add the egg yolks and milk and beat just until blended. Do *not* overbeat; that would leave too much air in the mixture. Once everything is blended, *stop*. Stir in the walnuts and vanilla. Gently fold in the beaten egg whites.
5. Divide the batter equally among the prepared cake pans. Smooth the tops and bake for 25 minutes, or until golden brown. Transfer to wire racks and let cool completely.
6. Prepare the icing: In a medium saucepan over medium heat, melt the butter. Add the cream and heat until the mixture is slightly less than boiling. Remove from heat. Add the powdered sugar and whisk until completely smooth. Add the vanilla.
7. When you are certain the cake layers are completely cooled, peel off the waxed paper and frost the cake. Place the first layer, top side down, on a cake plate and spread evenly with icing. Top with another layer, top side down, and repeat until

all four layers are stacked. Use the remaining icing to cover the top and sides of the cake.

8. Place the iced cake in an airtight container and leave it completely undisturbed for five days before serving. At the end of the five days, all the flavors of the cake will have matured, and you'll understand why the long wait was worth it when you take your first bite.

Bûche de Noël (Christmas Log Cake)

From France

PREPARE: *45 minutes plus 30 minutes for chilling* • BAKE: *15 minutes*

SERVES: *8*

On Christmas Eve in France, families attend Midnight Mass and then hurry home for *réveillon*, a repast that everyone looks forward to all year long. Goose may be served, or turkey; some regions favor seafood. But it's a given that almost every *réveillon* will conclude with *Bûche de Noël*, the amazing cake that has been the crowning glory of French holiday feasts for centuries. In and of itself, *Bûche de Noël* is a wonder, but in Christmas history it represents more than dessert. The name and shape of this sweet delight pays tribute to perhaps the oldest winter holiday tradition of all.

Ancient cultures celebrated the winter solstice (the shortest day of the year) by burning the trunk of a large tree to symbolize their thanks for previous warm seasons and their plea for more to follow. As the Christian Church expanded and essentially absorbed some pagan customs, log burning was incorporated into Christmas festivities. Some people placed one end of a log in their fireplace and pushed it in a bit farther each day until the log was completely turned to ashes on December 25.

In more modern times, people everywhere, but particularly in France (I couldn't tell you why), began to find log burning inconvenient. The French cities of Lyons and Paris disagree over whose townspeople first decided to bake a Christmas cake in the shape of a yule log and celebrate the holiday by eating "logs" rather than burning them. But by the late 1800s *Bûche de Noël* had found its way onto the menu of almost every French family's *réveillon*.

It should be part of your holiday tradition, too, since the dish combines Christmas history with exceptional delectability. Lars serves *Bûche de Noël* to conclude every North Pole Christmas Eve dinner; it wouldn't seem like the real holiday to us without it. I personally can never get enough. Should you happen to bake *Bûche de Noël* this Christmas, please interrupt your meal to answer that knock on your door. It's probably me hoping for an invitation to join you for dessert!

Lars Says: *"Santa's not joking. He'd eat a whole* Bûche de Noël *by himself if Mrs. Claus allowed it, which of course she won't. This is a rich, delicious dish, and one slice ought to be plenty to satisfy any appetite, including his.*

"There are several flavor variations, and I'm presenting here the instructions for a vanilla cake with chocolate buttercream frosting. A popular alternative in France is chocolate cake with coffee buttercream icing, so I'm also noting some additional steps if you think your family or friends would prefer that variation. Santa—and the rest of us—love both!

"If you don't have an electric mixer, you can use a handheld mixer to make the frosting."

THE CAKE:

³/₄ cup granulated sugar
4 eggs, separated
1 tsp. vanilla extract
pinch of cream of tartar
³/₄ cup cake flour, sifted

(To make a chocolate cake, add *¹/₄ cup alkalized cocoa powder* and sift it with the cake flour. Add the cocoa powder/cake flour mixture by dividing it in half and gently folding both batches into the egg mixture.)

THE BUTTERCREAM FROSTING:

4 large egg whites
1 cup sugar
1¹/₂ cups (3 sticks) unsalted butter, room temperature
2 ozs. semisweet chocolate, cut into small, thin slices
2 ozs. unsweetened chocolate, cut into small, thin slices

(To make coffee buttercream frosting, use *2 tbsp. instant espresso powder* and *2 tbsp. rum* instead of the semisweet and unsweetened chocolate pieces. Whisk the espresso powder and rum into the buttercream.)

1. Preheat your oven to 375°F. Grease the bottom of a 15 by 10–inch baking pan and line with parchment paper; set aside.

2. Remove 2 tbsp. of the sugar from the ¾ cup called for in this recipe and set aside. In a large bowl, beat the egg yolks and the remaining sugar until blended. Add the vanilla and beat until thoroughly mixed.

3. In a separate bowl, beat the egg whites and the cream of tartar until the mixture holds soft peaks when the beaters are lifted. Add the reserved 2 tbsp. sugar and beat until the egg whites are glossy and hold stiff peaks.

4. In two additions, gently fold the flour into the egg yolk mixture. Add one-quarter of the beaten egg whites. Then fold in the remaining egg whites. Pour the batter into the prepared pan, spreading it evenly into the corners. Bake for 15 minutes.

5. While the cake is baking, spread a dish towel flat on your kitchen counter. Lay a piece of parchment paper slightly larger than the cake on top of the towel. Sprinkle the paper with sugar.

6. When the cake is done, invert it onto the paper on top of the towel, lining up the cake with the sides of the paper as closely as you can. Then gently peel off the parchment. Beginning at one shorter end of the cake, slowly roll up the cake with the new parchment paper still inside. Wrap the dish towel around the cake, place it on a wire rack, and let cool.

7. While the cake is cooling, make the frosting: Using an electric mixer, blend the egg whites and sugar in a large bowl. Set the bowl over a pot of simmering water and whisk gently until the sugar has dissolved and the egg whites are hot. Attach the bowl to the mixer and whip with the whisk on medium speed until cooled.

8. Switch to the paddle attachment and beat in the softened butter. Continue beating until the buttercream is smooth. Then add the semisweet and unsweetened choco-late pieces and whisk until melted and smooth.

9. When the cake has completely cooled, unroll it. Spread the frosting evenly over

the top. Roll the cake up again, removing the parchment paper from the bottom as you roll. Cover the cake loosely and refrigerate for 30 minutes.

10. Just before serving, you can do some things to lend an even more yule log–like appearance to the cake. For instance, spread leftover frosting over the sides, then run the tines of a fork over the frosting to create the illusion of bark. Dust the top of the cake with powdered sugar to symbolize snow and the winter solstice. Cut off a small piece at an angle from one end of the "log" and attach it to the side with some frosting to resemble a bough.

ACKNOWLEDGMENTS

Santa and Lars could not have compiled their cookbook without the critical input of North Pole assistant chefs Larry Wilson, Andrea Ahles Koos, and Grant Skokan-Guinn.

We appreciate the willingness of Attila, Saint Francis, Leonardo da Vinci, Layla, Theodore Roosevelt, and Willie Skokan to share their favorite holiday recipes.

Thanks also to Sara Carder, Joel Fotinos, Shanta Small, Laura Ingman, Katherine Obertance, Jim Donovan, Christopher Radko, Phyllis Stone, Barry Shlachter, Hannelore Paasch, Guille Fernandez, Scott and Julie Nishimura, Jim Firth, Frank Lauden, Robert Fernandez, Joseph Koos, Yelena Koos, and Alexander Koos.

Everything I write is always for Nora, Adam, and Grant.

INDEX

The Christmas Chronicles
by Jeff Guinn
More than 275,000 copies sold

The Autobiography of Santa Claus

"A book that deserves classic status."

—*The Dallas Morning News*

Santa's autobiography combines solid historical fact with glorious legend to deliver the definitive story of Santa Claus. Families will delight in each chapter of this Christmas classic— one per cold December night leading up to Christmas!

ISBN 978-58542-265-4 (hardcover)
ISBN 978-1-58542-448-1 (trade paper)

How Mrs. Claus Saved Christmas

Rich in historical detail, adventure, and plain ol' Christmas fun. The first lady of Christmas recounts the seventeenth-century story of how she and a very brave group of people battled against England's Parliament and marched through the streets of Canterbury to save the treasured holiday from being lost forever.

ISBN 978-1-58542-437-5 (hardcover)
ISBN 978-1-58542-535-8 (trade paper)

The Great Santa Search

In this delightful holiday tale, Santa himself takes readers on a sleigh ride through the history of Christmas in America, from the first Kris Kringle impersonator, hired in 1841 to lure shoppers into a dry goods store, to 2006, as a new reality TV show featuring a competition to find the "real" Saint Nicholas threatens to destroy the true spirit of Christmas.

ISBN 978-1-58542-513-6 (hardcover)
ISBN 978-1-58542-599-0 (trade paper)